PRONUNCIATION

Letter	Serbian example	T&P phonetic alphabet	English example

Vowels

Letter	Serbian example	T&P phonetic alphabet	English example
А а	авлија	[a]	shorter than in ask
Е е	ексер	[e]	elm, medal
И и	излаз	[i]	shorter than in feet
О о	очи	[o]	pod, John
У у	ученик	[u]	book

Consonants

Letter	Serbian example	T&P phonetic alphabet	English example
Б б	брег	[b]	baby, book
В в	вода	[ʋ]	vase, winter
Г г	глава	[g]	game, gold
Д д	дим	[d]	day, doctor
Ђ ђ	ђак	[ʤ]	jeans, gene
Ж ж	жица	[ʒ]	forge, pleasure
З з	зец	[z]	zebra, please
Ј ј	мој	[j]	yes, New York
К к	киша	[k]	clock, kiss
Л л	лептир	[l]	lace, people
Љ љ	љиљан	[ʎ]	daily, million
М м	мајка	[m]	magic, milk
Н н	нос	[n]	name, normal
Њ њ	књига	[ɲ]	canyon, new
П п	праг	[p]	pencil, private
Р р	рука	[r]	rice, radio
С с	слово	[s]	city, boss
Т т	тело	[t]	tourist, trip
Ћ ћ	ћуран	[tɕ]	cheer
Ф ф	фењер	[f]	face, food
Х х	хлеб	[h]	home, have
Ц ц	цео	[ts]	cats, tsetse fly
Ч ч	чизме	[ʧ]	church, French

Letter	Serbian example	T&P phonetic alphabet	English example
Џ џ	џбун	[ʤ]	joke, general
Ш ш	шах	[ʃ]	machine, shark

LIST OF ABBREVIATIONS

English abbreviations

ab.	-	about
adj	-	adjective
adv	-	adverb
anim.	-	animate
as adj	-	attributive noun used as adjective
e.g.	-	for example
etc.	-	et cetera
fam.	-	familiar
fem.	-	feminine
form.	-	formal
inanim.	-	inanimate
masc.	-	masculine
math	-	mathematics
mil.	-	military
n	-	noun
pl	-	plural
pron.	-	pronoun
sb	-	somebody
sing.	-	singular
sth	-	something
v aux	-	auxiliary verb
vi	-	intransitive verb
vi, vt	-	intransitive, transitive verb
vt	-	transitive verb

Serbian abbreviations

ж	-	feminine noun
ж мн	-	feminine plural
м	-	masculine noun
м мн	-	masculine plural
мн	-	plural
с	-	neuter
с мн	-	neuter plural

SERBIAN
PHRASEBOOK

This section contains
important phrases that may
come in handy in various
real-life situations.
The phrasebook will help
you ask for directions, clarify
a price, buy tickets, and
order food at a restaurant

T&P Books Publishing

PHRASEBOOK
CONTENTS

T&P Books Publishing

The bare minimum

Excuse me, …	**Извините, …** Izvinite, …
Hello.	**Добар дан.** Dobar dan
Thank you.	**Хвала вам.** Hvala vam
Good bye.	**Довиђења.** Doviđenja
Yes.	**Да.** Da
No.	**Не.** Ne
I don't know.	**Не знам.** Ne znam
Where? | Where to? | When?	**Где? | Куда? | Када?** Gde? | Kuda? | Kada?

I need …	**Треба ми …** Treba mi …
I want …	**Хоћу …** Hoću …
Do you have …?	**Имате ли …?** Imate li …?
Is there a … here?	**Да ли овде постоји …?** Da li ovde postoji …?
May I …?	**Смем ли …?** Smem li …?
…, please (polite request)	**молим** molim

I'm looking for …	**Тражим …** Tražim …
restroom	**тоалет** toalet
ATM	**банкомат** bankomat
pharmacy (drugstore)	**апотеку** apoteku
hospital	**болницу** bolnicu
police station	**полицијску станицу** policijsku stanicu
subway	**метро** metro

taxi	**такси** taksi
train station	**железничку станицу** železničku stanicu

My name is …	**Ја се зовем …** Ja se zovem …
What's your name?	**Како се ви зовете?** Kako se vi zovete?
Could you please help me?	**Да ли бисте, молим вас, могли да ми помогнете?** Da li biste, molim vas, mogli da mi pomognete?
I've got a problem.	**Имам проблем.** Imam problem
I don't feel well.	**Не осећам се добро.** Ne osećam se dobro
Call an ambulance!	**Позовите хитну помоћ!** Pozovite hitnu pomoć!
May I make a call?	**Смем ли да телефонирам?** Smem li da telefoniram?

I'm sorry.	**Извините …** Izvinite …
You're welcome.	**Нема на чему.** Nema na čemu

I, me	**ја, мене** ja, mene
you (inform.)	**ти** ti
he	**он** on
she	**она** ona
they (masc.)	**они** oni
they (fem.)	**оне** one
we	**ми** mi
you (pl)	**ви** vi
you (sg, form.)	**ви** vi

ENTRANCE	**УЛАЗ** ULAZ
EXIT	**ИЗЛАЗ** IZLAZ
OUT OF ORDER	**НЕ РАДИ** NE RADI

CLOSED	**ЗАТВОРЕНО** ZATVORENO
OPEN	**ОТВОРЕНО** OTVORENO
FOR WOMEN	**ЗА ЖЕНЕ** ZA ŽENE
FOR MEN	**ЗА МУШКАРЦЕ** ZA MUŠKARCE

Questions

Where?	**Где?** Gde?
Where to?	**Куда?** Kuda?
Where from?	**Одакле?** Odakle?
Why?	**Зашто?** Zašto?
For what reason?	**Из ког разлога?** Iz kog razloga?
When?	**Када?** Kada?
How long?	**Колико дуго?** Koliko dugo?
At what time?	**У колико сати?** U koliko sati?
How much?	**Колико?** Koliko?
Do you have …?	**Имате ли …?** Imate li …?
Where is …?	**Где се налази …?** Gde se nalazi …?
What time is it?	**Колико је сати?** Koliko je sati?
May I make a call?	**Смем ли да телефонирам?** Smem li da telefoniram?
Who's there?	**Ко је тамо?** Ko je tamo?
Can I smoke here?	**Да ли се овде пуши?** Da li se ovde puši?
May I …?	**Смем ли …?** Smem li …?

Needs

I'd like ...	**Волео /Волела/ бих ...** Voleo /Volela/ bih ...
I don't want ...	**Не желим ...** Ne želim ...
I'm thirsty.	**Жедан /Жедна/ сам.** Žedan /Žedna/ sam.
I want to sleep.	**Хоћу да спавам.** Hoću da spavam
I want ...	**Хоћу ...** Hoću ...
to wash up	**да се освежим** da se osvežim
to brush my teeth	**да оперем зубе** da operem zube
to rest a while	**да се мало одморим** da se malo odmorim
to change my clothes	**да се пресвучем** da se presvučem
to go back to the hotel	**да се вратим у хотел** da se vratim u hotel
to buy ...	**да купим ...** da kupim ...
to go to ...	**да идем до ...** da idem do ...
to visit ...	**да посетим ...** da posetim ...
to meet with ...	**да се нађем са ...** da se nađem sa ...
to make a call	**да телефонирам** da telefoniram
I'm tired.	**Уморан /Уморна/ сам.** Umoran /Umorna/ sam
We are tired.	**Ми смо уморни.** Mi smo umorni
I'm cold.	**Хладно ми је.** Hladno mi je
I'm hot.	**Вруће ми је.** Vruće mi je
I'm OK.	**Добро сам.** Dobro sam

I need to make a call.	**Треба да телефонирам.** Treba da telefoniram
I need to go to the restroom.	**Морам до тоалета.** Moram do toaleta
I have to go.	**Морам да идем.** Moram da idem
I have to go now.	**Морам одмах да идем.** Moram odmah da idem

Asking for directions

Excuse me, ...	**Извините ...** Izvinite ...
Where is ...?	**Где се налази ...?** Gde se nalazi ...?
Which way is ...?	**Куда до ...?** Kuda do ...?
Could you help me, please?	**Можете ли ми, молим вас, помоћи?** Možete li mi, molim vas, pomoći?
I'm looking for ...	**Тражим ...** Tražim ...
I'm looking for the exit.	**Тражим излаз.** Tražim izlaz
I'm going to ...	**Идем до ...** Idem do ...
Am I going the right way to ...?	**Јесам ли на правом путу до ...?** Jesam li na pravom putu do ...?
Is it far?	**Да ли је далеко?** Da li je daleko?
Can I get there on foot?	**Могу ли до тамо пешке?** Mogu li do tamo peške?
Can you show me on the map?	**Можете ли да ми покажете на мапи?** Možete li da mi pokažete na mapi?
Show me where we are right now.	**Покажите ми где смо ми сада.** Pokažite mi gde smo mi sada
Here	**Овде** Ovde
There	**Тамо** Tamo
This way	**Овим путем** Ovim putem
Turn right.	**Скрените десно.** Skrenite desno
Turn left.	**Скрените лево.** Skrenite levo
first (second, third) turn	**прво (друго, треће) скретање** prvo (drugo, treće) skretanje

to the right	**десно** desno
to the left	**лево** levo
Go straight ahead.	**Идите само право.** Idite samo pravo

Signs

WELCOME!	**ДОБРОДОШЛИ!** DOBRODOŠLI!
ENTRANCE	**УЛАЗ** ULAZ
EXIT	**ИЗЛАЗ** IZLAZ
PUSH	**ГУРАЈ** GURAJ
PULL	**ВУЦИ** VUCI
OPEN	**ОТВОРЕНО** OTVORENO
CLOSED	**ЗАТВОРЕНО** ZATVORENO
FOR WOMEN	**ЗА ЖЕНЕ** ZA ŽENE
FOR MEN	**ЗА МУШКАРЦЕ** ZA MUŠKARCE
GENTLEMEN, GENTS (m)	**МУШКАРЦИ** MUŠKARCI
WOMEN (f)	**ЖЕНЕ** ŽENE
DISCOUNTS	**ПРОДАЈА** PRODAJA
SALE	**РАСПРОДАЈА** RASPRODAJA
FREE	**БЕСПЛАТНО** BESPLATNO
NEW!	**НОВО!** NOVO!
ATTENTION!	**ПАЖЊА!** PAŽNJA!
NO VACANCIES	**НЕМА СЛОБОДНИХ МЕСТА** NEMA SLOBODNIH MESTA
RESERVED	**РЕЗЕРВИСАНО** REZERVISANO
ADMINISTRATION	**АДМИНИСТРАЦИЈА** ADMINISTRACIJA
STAFF ONLY	**САМО ЗА ЗАПОСЛЕНЕ** SAMO ZA ZAPOSLENE

BEWARE OF THE DOG!	**ПАС УЈЕДА!** PAS UJEDA!
NO SMOKING!	**ЗАБРАЊЕНО ПУШЕЊЕ!** ZABRANJENO PUŠENJE!
DO NOT TOUCH!	**НЕ ПИПАЈ!** NE PIPAJ!
DANGEROUS	**ОПАСНО** OPASNO
DANGER	**ОПАСНОСТ** OPASNOST
HIGH VOLTAGE	**ВИСОК НАПОН** VISOK NAPON
NO SWIMMING!	**ЗАБРАЊЕНО ПЛИВАЊЕ!** ZABRANJENO PLIVANJE!

OUT OF ORDER	**НЕ РАДИ** NE RADI
FLAMMABLE	**ЗАПАЉИВО** ZAPALJIVO
FORBIDDEN	**ЗАБРАЊЕНО** ZABRANJENO
NO TRESPASSING!	**ЗАБРАЊЕН ПРОЛАЗ!** ZABRANJEN PROLAZ!
WET PAINT	**СВЕЖЕ ОКРЕЧЕНО** SVEŽE OKREČENO

CLOSED FOR RENOVATIONS	**ЗАТВОРЕНО ЗБОГ РЕНОВИРАЊА** ZATVORENO ZBOG RENOVIRANJA
WORKS AHEAD	**РАДОВИ НА ПУТУ** RADOVI NA PUTU
DETOUR	**ОБИЛАЗАК** OBILAZAK

Transportation. General phrases

plane	**авион**
	avion
train	**воз**
	voz
bus	**аутобус**
	autobus
ferry	**трајект**
	trajekt
taxi	**такси**
	taksi
car	**ауто**
	auto

schedule	**ред вожње**
	red vožnje
Where can I see the schedule?	**Где могу да видим ред вожње?**
	Gde mogu da vidim red vožnje?
workdays (weekdays)	**радни дани**
	radni dani
weekends	**викенди**
	vikendi
holidays	**празници**
	praznici

DEPARTURE	**ОДЛАЗАК**
	ODLAZAK
ARRIVAL	**ДОЛАЗАК**
	DOLAZAK
DELAYED	**КАСНИ**
	KASNI
CANCELLED	**ОТКАЗАН**
	OTKAZAN

next (train, etc.)	**следећи**
	sledeći
first	**први**
	prvi
last	**последњи**
	poslednji

When is the next ...?	**Када је следећи ...?**
	Kada je sledeći ...?
When is the first ...?	**Када је први ...?**
	Kada je prvi ...?

When is the last …?

Када је последњи …?
Kada je poslednji …?

transfer (change of trains, etc.)

преседање
presedanje

to make a transfer

имати преседање
imati presedanje

Do I need to make a transfer?

Треба ли да преседам?
Treba li da presedam?

Buying tickets

Where can I buy tickets?	**Где могу да купим карте?** Gde mogu da kupim karte?
ticket	**карта** karta
to buy a ticket	**купити карту** kupiti kartu
ticket price	**цена карте** cena karte
Where to?	**Куда?** Kuda?
To what station?	**До које станице?** Do koje stanice?
I need ...	**Треба ми ...** Treba mi ...
one ticket	**једна карта** jedna karta
two tickets	**две карте** dve karte
three tickets	**три карте** tri karte
one-way	**у једном правцу** u jednom pravcu
round-trip	**повратна** povratna
first class	**прва класа** prva klasa
second class	**друга класа** druga klasa
today	**данас** danas
tomorrow	**сутра** sutra
the day after tomorrow	**прекосутра** prekosutra
in the morning	**ујутру** ujutru
in the afternoon	**после подне** posle podne
in the evening	**увече** uveče

aisle seat	**седиште до пролаза** sedište do prolaza
window seat	**седиште поред прозора** sedište pored prozora
How much?	**Колико?** Koliko?
Can I pay by credit card?	**Могу ли да платим кредитном картицом?** Mogu li da platim kreditnom karticom?

Bus

bus	**Аутобус** Autobus
intercity bus	**међуградски аутобус** međugradski autobus
bus stop	**аутобуска станица** autobuska stanica
Where's the nearest bus stop?	**Где је најближа аутобуска станица?** Gde je najbliža autobuska stanica?
number (bus ~, etc.)	**број** broj
Which bus do I take to get to ...?	**Којим аутобусом стижем до ...?** Kojim autobusom stižem do ...?
Does this bus go to ...?	**Да ли овај аутобус иде до ...?** Da li ovaj autobus ide do ...?
How frequent are the buses?	**Колико често иду аутобуси?** Koliko često idu autobusi?
every 15 minutes	**сваких 15 минута** svakih 15 minuta
every half hour	**сваких пола сата** svakih pola sata
every hour	**сваки сат** svaki sat
several times a day	**неколико пута дневно** nekoliko puta dnevno
... times a day	**... пута дневно** ... puta dnevno
schedule	**ред вожње** red vožnje
Where can I see the schedule?	**Где могу да видим ред вожње?** Gde mogu da vidim red vožnje?
When is the next bus?	**Када је следећи аутобус?** Kada je sledeći autobus?
When is the first bus?	**Када је први аутобус?** Kada je prvi autobus?
When is the last bus?	**Када је последњи аутобус?** Kada je poslednji autobus?
stop	**станица** stanica
next stop	**следећа станица** sledeća stanica

last stop (terminus)

последња станица
poslednja stanica

Stop here, please.

Станите овде, молим вас.
Stanite ovde, molim vas

Excuse me, this is my stop.

Извините, ово је моја станица.
Izvinite, ovo je moja stanica

Train

train	**воз** voz
suburban train	**приградски воз** prigradski voz
long-distance train	**међуградски воз** međugradski voz
train station	**железничка станица** železnička stanica
Excuse me, where is the exit to the platform?	**Извините, где је излаз до перона?** Izvinite, gde je izlaz do perona?
Does this train go to …?	**Да ли овај воз иде до …?** Da li ovaj voz ide do …?
next train	**следећи воз** sledeći voz
When is the next train?	**Када полази следећи воз?** Kada polazi sledeći voz?
Where can I see the schedule?	**Где могу да видим ред вожње?** Gde mogu da vidim red vožnje?
From which platform?	**Са ког перона?** Sa kog perona?
When does the train arrive in …?	**Када воз стиже у …?** Kada voz stiže u …?
Please help me.	**Молим вас, помозите ми.** Molim vas, pomozite mi
I'm looking for my seat.	**Тражим своје место.** Tražim svoje mesto
We're looking for our seats.	**Ми тражимо своја места.** Mi tražimo svoja mesta
My seat is taken.	**Моје место је заузето.** Moje mesto je zauzeto
Our seats are taken.	**Наша места су заузета.** Naša mesta su zauzeta
I'm sorry but this is my seat.	**Извините, али ово је моје место.** Izvinite, ali ovo je moje mesto
Is this seat taken?	**Да ли је ово место заузето?** Da li je ovo mesto zauzeto?
May I sit here?	**Могу ли овде да седнем?** Mogu li ovde da sednem?

On the train. Dialogue (No ticket)

Ticket, please.	**Карту, молим вас.** Kartu, molim vas
I don't have a ticket.	**Немам карту.** Nemam kartu
I lost my ticket.	**Изгубио сам карту.** Izgubio sam kartu
I forgot my ticket at home.	**Заборавио сам карту код куће.** Zaboravio sam kartu kod kuće
You can buy a ticket from me.	**Од мене можете купити карту.** Od mene možete kupiti kartu
You will also have to pay a fine.	**Такође ћете морати да платите казну.** Takođe ćete morati da platite kaznu
Okay.	**У реду.** U redu
Where are you going?	**Где идете?** Gde idete?
I'm going to …	**Идем до …** Idem do …
How much? I don't understand.	**Колико? Не разумем.** Koliko? Ne razumem
Write it down, please.	**Напишите, молим вас.** Napišite, molim vas
Okay. Can I pay with a credit card?	**У реду. Да ли могу да платим кредитном картицом?** U redu. Da li mogu da platim kreditnom karticom?
Yes, you can.	**Да, можете.** Da, možete
Here's your receipt.	**Изволите рачун.** Izvolite račun
Sorry about the fine.	**Извините због казне.** Izvinite zbog kazne
That's okay. It was my fault.	**У реду је. Моја грешка.** U redu je. Moja greška
Enjoy your trip.	**Уживајте у путовању.** Uživajte u putovanju

Taxi

taxi	**такси** taksi
taxi driver	**таксиста** taksista
to catch a taxi	**ухватити такси** uhvatiti taksi
taxi stand	**такси станица** taksi stanica
Where can I get a taxi?	**Где могу да нађем такси?** Gde mogu da nađem taksi?
to call a taxi	**позвати такси** pozvati taksi
I need a taxi.	**Треба ми такси.** Treba mi taksi
Right now.	**Одмах.** Odmah
What is your address (location)?	**Која је ваша адреса?** Koja je vaša adresa?
My address is …	**Моја адреса је …** Moja adresa je …
Your destination?	**Докле идете?** Dokle idete?
Excuse me, …	**Извините …** Izvinite …
Are you available?	**Да ли сте слободни?** Da li ste slobodni?
How much is it to get to …?	**Колико кошта до …?** Koliko košta do …?
Do you know where it is?	**Да ли знате где је?** Da li znate gde je?
Airport, please.	**Аеродром, молим.** Aerodrom, molim
Stop here, please.	**Станите овде, молим вас.** Stanite ovde, molim vas
It's not here.	**Није овде.** Nije ovde
This is the wrong address.	**Ово је погрешна адреса.** Ovo je pogrešna adresa
Turn left.	**скрените лево** skrenite levo
Turn right.	**скрените десно** skrenite desno

How much do I owe you?	**Колико вам дугујем?** Koliko vam dugujem?
I'd like a receipt, please.	**Рачун, молим.** Račun, molim
Keep the change.	**Задржите кусур.** Zadržite kusur

Would you please wait for me?	**Да ли бисте ме сачекали, молим вас?** Da li biste me sačekali, molim vas?
five minutes	**пет минута** pet minuta
ten minutes	**десет минута** deset minuta
fifteen minutes	**петнаест минута** petnaest minuta
twenty minutes	**двадесет минута** dvadeset minuta
half an hour	**пола сата** pola sata

Hotel

Hello.	**Добар дан.** Dobar dan
My name is …	**Ja се зовем …** Ja se zovem …
I have a reservation.	**Имам резервацију.** Imam rezervaciju
I need …	**Треба ми …** Treba mi …
a single room	**једнокреветна соба** jednokrevetna soba
a double room	**двокреветна соба** dvokrevetna soba
How much is that?	**Колико је то?** Koliko je to?
That's a bit expensive.	**То је мало скупо.** To je malo skupo
Do you have anything else?	**Да ли имате неку другу могућност?** Da li imate neku drugu mogućnost?
I'll take it.	**Узећу то.** Uzeću to
I'll pay in cash.	**Платићу готовином.** Platiću gotovinom
I've got a problem.	**Имам проблем.** Imam problem
My … is broken.	**Мој … је сломљен /Moja… je сломљена/.** Moj … je slomljen /slomljena/
My … is out of order.	**Мој /Moja/ … не ради.** Moj /Moja/ … ne radi
TV	**телевизор (м)** televizor
air conditioner	**клима уређај (м)** klima uređaj
tap	**славина (ж)** slavina
shower	**туш (м)** tuš
sink	**лавабо (м)** lavabo

safe	**сеф (м)** sef
door lock	**брава (ж)** brava
electrical outlet	**електрична утичница (ж)** električna utičnica
hairdryer	**фен (м)** fen

I don't have …	**Немам …** Nemam …
water	**воде** vode
light	**светла** svetla
electricity	**струје** struje

Can you give me …?	**Можете ли ми дати …?** Možete li mi dati …?
a towel	**пешкир** peškir
a blanket	**ћебе** ćebe
slippers	**папуче** papuče
a robe	**баде-мантил** bade-mantil
shampoo	**мало шампона** malo šampona
soap	**мало сапуна** malo sapuna

I'd like to change rooms.	**Хоћу да заменим собу.** Hoću da zamenim sobu
I can't find my key.	**Не могу да нађем свој кључ.** Ne mogu da nađem svoj ključ
Could you open my room, please?	**Можете ли ми отворити собу, молим вас?** Možete li mi otvoriti sobu, molim vas?
Who's there?	**Ко је тамо?** Ko je tamo?
Come in!	**Уђите!** Uđite!
Just a minute!	**Само тренутак!** Samo trenutak!

Not right now, please.	**Не сада, молим вас.** Ne sada, molim vas
Come to my room, please.	**Дођите у моју собу, молим вас.** Dođite u moju sobu, molim vas

I'd like to order food service.

Хтео бих да поручим храну.
Hteo bih da poručim hranu

My room number is …

Број моје собе је …
Broj moje sobe je …

I'm leaving …

Одлазим …
Odlazim …

We're leaving …

Ми одлазимо …
Mi odlazimo …

right now

одмах
odmah

this afternoon

овог поподнева
ovog popodneva

tonight

вечерас
večeras

tomorrow

сутра
sutra

tomorrow morning

сутра ујутру
sutra ujutru

tomorrow evening

сутра увече
sutra uveče

the day after tomorrow

прекосутра
prekosutra

I'd like to pay.

Хтео бих да платим.
Hteo bih da platim

Everything was wonderful.

Све је било дивно.
Sve je bilo divno

Where can I get a taxi?

Где могу да нађем такси?
Gde mogu da nađem taksi?

Would you call a taxi for me, please?

Да ли бисте ми позвали такси, молим вас?
Da li biste mi pozvali taksi, molim vas?

Restaurant

Can I look at the menu, please?	**Могу ли да погледам мени, молим вас?** Mogu li da pogledam meni, molim vas?
Table for one.	**Сто за једног.** Sto za jednog
There are two (three, four) of us.	**Има нас двоје (троје, четворо).** Ima nas dvoje (troje, četvoro)

Smoking	**За пушаче** Za pušače
No smoking	**За непушаче** Za nepušače
Excuse me! (addressing a waiter)	**Конобар!** Konobar!
menu	**мени** meni
wine list	**винска карта** vinska karta
The menu, please.	**Мени, молим вас.** Meni, molim vas

Are you ready to order?	**Да ли сте спремни да наручите?** Da li ste spremni da naručite?
What will you have?	**Шта бисте хтели?** Šta biste hteli?
I'll have ...	**Ја ћу ...** Ja ću ...

I'm a vegetarian.	**Ја сам вегетеријанац /вегетаријанка/.** Ja sam vegeterijanac /vegetarijanka/
meat	**месо** meso
fish	**рибу** ribu
vegetables	**поврће** povrće
Do you have vegetarian dishes?	**Имате ли вегетеријанска јела?** Imate li vegeterijanska jela?
I don't eat pork.	**Не једем свињетину.** Ne jedem svinjetinu

| He /she/ doesn't eat meat. | **Он /Она/ не једе месо.**
On /Ona/ ne jede meso |
| I am allergic to ... | **Алергичан /Алергична/ сам на ...**
Alergičan /Alergična/ sam na ... |

Would you please bring me ...	**Да ли бисте ми, молим вас, донели ...** Da li biste mi, molim vas, doneli ...
salt | pepper | sugar	**со | бибер | шећер** so | biber | šećer
coffee | tea | dessert	**кафу | чај | дезерт** kafu | čaj | dezert
water | sparkling | plain	**воду | газирану | негазирану** vodu | gaziranu | negaziranu
a spoon | fork | knife	**кашику | виљушку | нож** kašiku | viljušku | nož
a plate | napkin	**тањир | салвету** tanjir | salvetu

Enjoy your meal!	**Пријатно!** Prijatno!
One more, please.	**Још једно, молим.** Još jedno, molim
It was very delicious.	**Било је изврсно.** Bilo je izvrsno

check | change | tip	**рачун | кусур | бакшиш** račun | kusur | bakšiš
Check, please. (Could I have the check, please?)	**Рачун, молим.** Račun, molim
Can I pay by credit card?	**Могу ли да платим кредитном картицом?** Mogu li da platim kreditnom karticom?
I'm sorry, there's a mistake here.	**Извините, овде је грешка.** Izvinite, ovde je greška

Shopping

Can I help you?	**Могу ли да вам помогнем?** Mogu li da vam pomognem?
Do you have ...?	**Имате ли ...?** Imate li ...?
I'm looking for ...	**Тражим ...** Tražim ...
I need ...	**Треба ми ...** Treba mi ...

I'm just looking.	**Само гледам.** Samo gledam
We're just looking.	**Само гледамо.** Samo gledamo
I'll come back later.	**Вратићу се касније.** Vratiću se kasnije
We'll come back later.	**Вратићемо се касније.** Vratićemo se kasnije
discounts	sale	**попусти	распродаја** popusti	rasprodaja

Would you please show me ...	**Да ли бисте ми, молим вас, показали ...** Da li biste mi, molim vas, pokazali ...
Would you please give me ...	**Да ли бисте ми, молим вас, дали ...** Da li biste mi, molim vas, dali ...
Can I try it on?	**Могу ли да пробам?** Mogu li da probam?
Excuse me, where's the fitting room?	**Извините, где је кабина за пресвлачење?** Izvinite, gde je kabina za presvlačenje?
Which color would you like?	**Коју боју бисте хтели?** Koju boju biste hteli?
size	length	**величина	дужина** veličina	dužina
How does it fit?	**Како ми стоји?** Kako mi stoji?

How much is it?	**Колико кошта?** Koliko košta?
That's too expensive.	**То је прескупо.** To je preskupo

I'll take it.	**Узећу то.** Uzeću to
Excuse me, where do I pay?	**Извините, где се плаћа?** Izvinite, gde se plaća?
Will you pay in cash or credit card?	**Плаћате ли готовином или кредитном картицом?** Plaćate li gotovinom ili kreditnom karticom?
In cash | with credit card	**Готовином | кредитном картицом** Gotovinom | kreditnom karticom

Do you want the receipt?	**Желите ли рачун?** Želite li račun?
Yes, please.	**Да, молим.** Da, molim
No, it's OK.	**Не, у реду је.** Ne, u redu je
Thank you. Have a nice day!	**Хвала. Пријатно!** Hvala. Prijatno!

In town

Excuse me, please.	**Извините, молим вас ...** Izvinite, molim vas ...
I'm looking for ...	**Тражим ...** Tražim ...

the subway	**метро** metro
my hotel	**свој хотел** svoj hotel
the movie theater	**биоскоп** bioskop
a taxi stand	**такси станицу** taksi stanicu

an ATM	**банкомат** bankomat
a foreign exchange office	**мењачницу** menjačnicu
an internet café	**интернет кафе** internet kafe
... street	**улицу ...** ulicu ...
this place	**ово место** ovo mesto

Do you know where ... is?	**Знате ли где је ...?** Znate li gde je ...?
Which street is this?	**Која је ово улица?** Koja je ovo ulica?

Show me where we are right now.	**Покажите ми где смо ми сада.** Pokažite mi gde smo mi sada
Can I get there on foot?	**Могу ли до тамо пешке?** Mogu li do tamo peške?
Do you have a map of the city?	**Имате ли мапу града?** Imate li mapu grada?

How much is a ticket to get in?	**Колико кошта улазница?** Koliko košta ulaznica?
Can I take pictures here?	**Могу ли овде да се сликам?** Mogu li ovde da se slikam?
Are you open?	**Да ли радите?** Da li radite?

When do you open?

Када отварате?
Kada otvarate?

When do you close?

Када затварате?
Kada zatvarate?

Money

money	**новац** novac
cash	**готовина** gotovina
paper money	**папирни новац** papirni novac
loose change	**кусур, ситниш** kusur, sitniš
check | change | tip	**рачун | кусур | бакшиш** račun | kusur | bakšiš
credit card	**кредитна картица** kreditna kartica
wallet	**новчаник** novčanik
to buy	**купити** kupiti
to pay	**платити** platiti
fine	**казна** kazna
free	**бесплатно** besplatno
Where can I buy ...?	**Где могу да купим ...?** Gde mogu da kupim ...?
Is the bank open now?	**Да ли је банка отворена сада?** Da li je banka otvorena sada?
When does it open?	**Када се отвара?** Kada se otvara?
When does it close?	**Када се затвара?** Kada se zatvara?
How much?	**Колико?** Koliko?
How much is this?	**Колико ово кошта?** Koliko ovo košta?
That's too expensive.	**То је прескупо.** To je preskupo
Excuse me, where do I pay?	**Извините, где се плаћа?** Izvinite, gde se plaća?
Check, please.	**Рачун, молим.** Račun, molim

Can I pay by credit card?	**Могу ли да платим кредитном картицом?** Mogu li da platim kreditnom karticom?
Is there an ATM here?	**Да ли овде негде има банкомат?** Da li ovde negde ima bankomat?
I'm looking for an ATM.	**Тражим банкомат.** Tražim bankomat

I'm looking for a foreign exchange office.	**Тражим мењачницу.** Tražim menjačnicu
I'd like to change …	**Хтео бих да заменим …** Hteo bih da zamenim …
What is the exchange rate?	**Колики је курс?** Koliki je kurs?
Do you need my passport?	**Да ли вам треба мој пасош?** Da li vam treba moj pasoš?

Time

What time is it?	**Колико је сати?** Koliko je sati?
When?	**Када?** Kada?
At what time?	**У колико сати?** U koliko sati?
now | later | after …	**сада | касније | после …** sada | kasnije | posle …
one o'clock	**један сат** jedan sat
one fifteen	**један и петнаест** jedan i petnaest
one thirty	**пола два** pola dva
one forty-five	**петнаест до два** petnaest do dva
one | two | three	**један | два | три** jedan | dva | tri
four | five | six	**четири | пет | шест** četiri | pet | šest
seven | eight | nine	**седам | осам | девет** sedam | osam | devet
ten | eleven | twelve	**десет | једанаест | дванаест** deset | jedanaest | dvanaest
in …	**за …** za …
five minutes	**пет минута** pet minuta
ten minutes	**десет минута** deset minuta
fifteen minutes	**петнаест минута** petnaest minuta
twenty minutes	**двадесет минута** dvadeset minuta
half an hour	**пола сата** pola sata
an hour	**сат времена** sat vremena

in the morning	**ујутру**
	ujutru
early in the morning	**рано ујутру**
	rano ujutru
this morning	**овог јутра**
	ovog jutra
tomorrow morning	**сутра ујутру**
	sutra ujutru
in the middle of the day	**за време ручка**
	za vreme ručka
in the afternoon	**после подне**
	posle podne
in the evening	**увече**
	uveče
tonight	**вечерас**
	večeras
at night	**ноћу**
	noću
yesterday	**јуче**
	juče
today	**данас**
	danas
tomorrow	**сутра**
	sutra
the day after tomorrow	**прекосутра**
	prekosutra
What day is it today?	**Који је данас дан?**
	Koji je danas dan?
It's ...	**Данас је ...**
	Danas je ...
Monday	**Понедељак**
	Ponedeljak
Tuesday	**Уторак**
	Utorak
Wednesday	**Среда**
	Sreda
Thursday	**Четвртак**
	Četvrtak
Friday	**Петак**
	Petak
Saturday	**Субота**
	Subota
Sunday	**Недеља**
	Nedelja

Greetings. Introductions

Hello.	**Здраво.** Zdravo
Pleased to meet you.	**Драго ми је што смо се упознали.** Drago mi je što smo se upoznali
Me too.	**И мени.** I meni
I'd like you to meet ...	**Хтео бих да упознаш ...** Hteo bih da upoznaš ...
Nice to meet you.	**Драго ми је што смо се упознали.** Drago mi je što smo se upoznali
How are you?	**Како сте?** Kako ste?
My name is ...	**Ja се зовем ...** Ja se zovem ...
His name is ...	**Он се зове ...** On se zove ...
Her name is ...	**Она се зове ...** Ona se zove ...
What's your name?	**Како се ви зовете?** Kako se vi zovete?
What's his name?	**Како се он зове?** Kako se on zove?
What's her name?	**Како се она зове?** Kako se ona zove?
What's your last name?	**Како се презивате?** Kako se prezivate?
You can call me ...	**Можете ме звати ...** Možete me zvati ...
Where are you from?	**Одакле сте?** Odakle ste?
I'm from ...	**Ja сам из ...** Ja sam iz ...
What do you do for a living?	**Чиме се бавите?** Čime se bavite?
Who is this?	**Ко је ово?** Ko je ovo?
Who is he?	**Ко је он?** Ko je on?
Who is she?	**Ко је она?** Ko je ona?

Who are they?	**Ко су они?** Ko su oni?
This is …	**Ово је …** Ovo je …
my friend (masc.)	**мој пријатељ** moj prijatelj
my friend (fem.)	**моја пријатељица** moja prijateljica
my husband	**мој муж** moj muž
my wife	**моја жена** moja žena
my father	**мој отац** moj otac
my mother	**моја мајка** moja majka
my brother	**мој брат** moj brat
my sister	**моја сестра** moja sestra
my son	**мој син** moj sin
my daughter	**моја ћерка** moja ćerka
This is our son.	**Ово је наш син.** Ovo je naš sin
This is our daughter.	**Ово је наша ћерка.** Ovo je naša ćerka
These are my children.	**Ово су моја деца.** Ovo su moja deca
These are our children.	**Ово су наша деца.** Ovo su naša deca

Farewells

Good bye!	**Довиђења!** Doviđenja!
Bye! (inform.)	**Ћао!** Ćao!
See you tomorrow.	**Видимо се сутра.** Vidimo se sutra
See you soon.	**Видимо се ускоро.** Vidimo se uskoro
See you at seven.	**Видимо се у седам.** Vidimo se u sedam
Have fun!	**Лепо се проведите!** Lepo se provedite!
Talk to you later.	**Чујемо се касније.** Čujemo se kasnije
Have a nice weekend.	**Леп викенд.** Lep vikend
Good night.	**Лаку ноћ.** Laku noć
It's time for me to go.	**Време је да кренем.** Vreme je da krenem
I have to go.	**Морам да кренем.** Moram da krenem
I will be right back.	**Одмах се враћам.** Odmah se vraćam
It's late.	**Касно је.** Kasno je
I have to get up early.	**Морам рано да устанем.** Moram rano da ustanem
I'm leaving tomorrow.	**Одлазим сутра.** Odlazim sutra
We're leaving tomorrow.	**Одлазимо сутра.** Odlazimo sutra
Have a nice trip!	**Лепо се проведите на путу!** Lepo se provedite na putu!
It was nice meeting you.	**Драго ми је што смо се упознали.** Drago mi je što smo se upoznali
It was nice talking to you.	**Драго ми је што смо поразговарали.** Drago mi je što smo porazgovarali
Thanks for everything.	**Хвала на свему.** Hvala na svemu

I had a very good time.	**Лепо сам се провео /провела/.** Lepo sam se proveo /provela/
We had a very good time.	**Лепо смо се провели.** Lepo smo se proveli
It was really great.	**Било је супер.** Bilo je super
I'm going to miss you.	**Недостајаћете ми.** Nedostajaćete mi
We're going to miss you.	**Недостајаћете нам.** Nedostajaćete nam

| Good luck! | **Срећно!**
Srećno! |
| Say hi to ... | **Поздравите ...**
Pozdravite ... |

Foreign language

I don't understand.	**Не разумем.** Ne razumem
Write it down, please.	**Можете ли то записати?** Možete li to zapisati?
Do you speak ...?	**Да ли говорите ...?** Da li govorite ...?

I speak a little bit of ...	**Помало говорим ...** Pomalo govorim ...
English	**Енглески** Engleski
Turkish	**Турски** Turski
Arabic	**Арапски** Arapski
French	**Француски** Francuski

German	**Немачки** Nemački
Italian	**Италијански** Italijanski
Spanish	**Шпански** Španski
Portuguese	**Португалски** Portugalski
Chinese	**Кинески** Kineski
Japanese	**Јапански** Japanski

Can you repeat that, please.	**Можете ли то да поновите, молим вас.** Možete li to da ponovite, molim vas
I understand.	**Разумем.** Razumem
I don't understand.	**Не разумем.** Ne razumem
Please speak more slowly.	**Молим вас, говорите спорије.** Molim vas, govorite sporije

Is that correct? (Am I saying it right?)   **Јел' тако?**
Jel' tako?

What is this? (What does this mean?)   **Шта је ово?**
Šta je ovo?

Apologies

Excuse me, please.	**Извините, молим вас.** Izvinite, molim vas
I'm sorry.	**Извините.** Izvinite
I'm really sorry.	**Jako ми је жао.** Jako mi je žao
Sorry, it's my fault.	**Извините, ја сам крив.** Izvinite, ja sam kriv
My mistake.	**Моja грешка.** Moja greška
May I ...?	**Смем ли ...?** Smem li ...?
Do you mind if I ...?	**Да ли би вам сметало да ...?** Da li bi vam smetalo da ...?
It's OK.	**OK je.** OK je
It's all right.	**У реду je.** U redu je
Don't worry about it.	**Не брините.** Ne brinite

Agreement

Yes.	**Да.** Da
Yes, sure.	**Да, свакако.** Da, svakako
OK (Good!)	**Добро, важи!** Dobro, važi!
Very well.	**Врло добро.** Vrlo dobro
Certainly!	**Свакако!** Svakako!
I agree.	**Слажем се.** Slažem se
That's correct.	**Тако је.** Tako je
That's right.	**То је тачно.** To je tačno
You're right.	**Ви сте у праву.** Vi ste u pravu
I don't mind.	**Не смета ми.** Ne smeta mi
Absolutely right.	**Потпуно тачно.** Potpuno tačno
It's possible.	**Могуће је.** Moguće je
That's a good idea.	**То је добра идеја.** To je dobra ideja
I can't say no.	**Не могу да одбијем.** Ne mogu da odbijem
I'd be happy to.	**Биће ми задовољство.** Biće mi zadovoljstvo
With pleasure.	**Са задовољством.** Sa zadovoljstvom

Refusal. Expressing doubt

No.	**Не.** Ne
Certainly not.	**Нипошто.** Nipošto
I don't agree.	**Не слажем се.** Ne slažem se
I don't think so.	**Не мислим тако.** Ne mislim tako
It's not true.	**Није истина.** Nije istina
You are wrong.	**Грешите.** Grešite
I think you are wrong.	**Мислим да грешите.** Mislim da grešite
I'm not sure.	**Нисам сигуран /сигурна/.** Nisam siguran /sigurna/
It's impossible.	**Немогуће.** Nemoguće
Nothing of the kind (sort)!	**Нема шансе!** Nema šanse!
The exact opposite.	**Потпуно супротно.** Potpuno suprotno
I'm against it.	**Ја сам против тога.** Ja sam protiv toga
I don't care.	**Баш ме брига.** Baš me briga
I have no idea.	**Немам појма.** Nemam pojma
I doubt it.	**Не мислим тако.** Ne mislim tako
Sorry, I can't.	**Жао ми је, не могу.** Žao mi je, ne mogu
Sorry, I don't want to.	**Жао ми је, не желим.** Žao mi je, ne želim
Thank you, but I don't need this.	**Хвала, али то ми није потребно.** Hvala, ali to mi nije potrebno
It's getting late.	**Већ је касно.** Već je kasno

I have to get up early.

Морам рано да устанем.
Moram rano da ustanem

I don't feel well.

Не осећам се добро.
Ne osećam se dobro

Expressing gratitude

Thank you.	**Хвала вам.** Hvala vam
Thank you very much.	**Много вам хвала.** Mnogo vam hvala
I really appreciate it.	**Заиста то ценим.** Zaista to cenim
I'm really grateful to you.	**Заиста сам вам захвалан /захвална/.** Zaista sam vam zahvalan /zahvalna/
We are really grateful to you.	**Заиста смо вам захвални.** Zaista smo vam zahvalni
Thank you for your time.	**Хвала вам на времену.** Hvala vam na vremenu
Thanks for everything.	**Хвала на свему.** Hvala na svemu
Thank you for ...	**Хвала вам на ...** Hvala vam na ...
your help	**вашој помоћи** vašoj pomoći
a nice time	**на лепом проводу** na lepom provodu
a wonderful meal	**лепом оброку** lepom obroku
a pleasant evening	**лепој вечери** lepoj večeri
a wonderful day	**дивном дану** divnom danu
an amazing journey	**сјајном путовању** sjajnom putovanju
Don't mention it.	**Није то ништа.** Nije to ništa
You are welcome.	**Нема на чему.** Nema na čemu
Any time.	**У свако доба.** U svako doba
My pleasure.	**Било ми је задовољство.** Bilo mi je zadovoljstvo
Forget it.	**Заборавите на то.** Zaboravite na to
Don't worry about it.	**Не брините за то.** Ne brinite za to

Congratulations. Best wishes

Congratulations!	**Честитам!** Čestitam!
Happy birthday!	**Срећан рођендан!** Srećan rođendan!
Merry Christmas!	**Срећан Божић!** Srećan Božić!
Happy New Year!	**Срећна Нова година!** Srećna Nova godina!
Happy Easter!	**Срећан Ускрс!** Srećan Uskrs!
Happy Hanukkah!	**Срећна Ханука!** Srećna Hanuka!
I'd like to propose a toast.	**Хтео бих да наздравим.** Hteo bih da nazdravim
Cheers!	**Живели!** Živeli!
Let's drink to …!	**Попијмо у име …!** Popijmo u ime …!
To our success!	**За наш успех!** Za naš uspeh!
To your success!	**За ваш успех!** Za vaš uspeh!
Good luck!	**Срећно!** Srećno!
Have a nice day!	**Пријатан дан!** Prijatan dan!
Have a good holiday!	**Уживајте на одмору!** Uživajte na odmoru!
Have a safe journey!	**Срећан пут!** Srećan put!
I hope you get better soon!	**Надам се да ћете се ускоро опоравити!** Nadam se da ćete se uskoro oporaviti!

Socializing

Why are you sad?	**Зашто си тужна?** Zašto si tužna?
Smile! Cheer up!	**Насмеши се! Разведри се!** Nasmeši se! Razvedri se!
Are you free tonight?	**Да ли си слободна вечерас?** Da li si slobodna večeras?
May I offer you a drink?	**Могу ли вам понудити пиће?** Mogu li vam ponuditi piće?
Would you like to dance?	**Да ли сте за плес?** Da li ste za ples?
Let's go to the movies.	**Хајдемо у биоскоп.** Hajdemo u bioskop
May I invite you to ...?	**Могу ли вас позвати у ...?** Mogu li vas pozvati u ...?
a restaurant	**ресторан** restoran
the movies	**биоскоп** bioskop
the theater	**позориште** pozorište
go for a walk	**у шетњу** u šetnju
At what time?	**У колико сати?** U koliko sati?
tonight	**вечерас** večeras
at six	**у шест** u šest
at seven	**у седам** u sedam
at eight	**у осам** u osam
at nine	**у девет** u devet
Do you like it here?	**Да ли ти се допада овде?** Da li ti se dopada ovde?
Are you here with someone?	**Да ли си овде са неким?** Da li si ovde sa nekim?
I'm with my friend.	**Са пријатељем /пријатељицом/.** Sa prijateljem /prijateljicom/

I'm with my friends.

Са пријатељима.
Sa prijateljima

No, I'm alone.

Не, сâм сам. /Не, сама сам/.
Ne, sâm sam. /Ne, sama sam/

Do you have a boyfriend?

Да ли имаш дечка?
Da li imaš dečka?

I have a boyfriend.

Имам дечка.
Imam dečka

Do you have a girlfriend?

Да ли имаш девојку?
Da li imaš devojku?

I have a girlfriend.

Имам девојку.
Imam devojku

Can I see you again?

Могу ли опет да те видим?
Mogu li opet da te vidim?

Can I call you?

Могу ли да те позовем?
Mogu li da te pozovem?

Call me. (Give me a call.)

Позови ме.
Pozovi me

What's your number?

Који ти је број телефона?
Koji ti je broj telefona?

I miss you.

Недостајеш ми.
Nedostaješ mi

You have a beautiful name.

Имате лепо име.
Imate lepo ime

I love you.

Волим те.
Volim te

Will you marry me?

Удај се за мене.
Udaj se za mene

You're kidding!

Шалите се!
Šalite se!

I'm just kidding.

Само се шалим.
Samo se šalim

Are you serious?

Да ли сте озбиљни?
Da li ste ozbiljni?

I'm serious.

Озбиљан сам.
Ozbiljan sam

Really?!

Стварно?!
Stvarno?!

It's unbelievable!

То је невероватно!
To je neverovatno!

I don't believe you.

Не верујем вам.
Ne verujem vam

I can't.

Не могу.
Ne mogu

I don't know.

Не знам.
Ne znam

I don't understand you.

Не разумем те.
Ne razumem te

Please go away.

Молим вас, одлазите.
Molim vas, odlazite

Leave me alone!

Оставите ме на миру!
Ostavite me na miru!

I can't stand him.

Не могу да га поднесем.
Ne mogu da ga podnesem

You are disgusting!

Одвратни сте!
Odvratni ste!

I'll call the police!

Зваћу полицију!
Zvaću policiju!

Sharing impressions. Emotions

I like it.	**Свиђа ми се то.** Sviđa mi se to
Very nice.	**Баш лепо.** Baš lepo
That's great!	**То је супер!** To je super!
It's not bad.	**Није лоше.** Nije loše
I don't like it.	**Не свиђа ми се.** Ne sviđa mi se
It's not good.	**Није добро.** Nije dobro
It's bad.	**Лоше је.** Loše je
It's very bad.	**Много је лоше.** Mnogo je loše
It's disgusting.	**Грозно је.** Grozno je
I'm happy.	**Срећан /Срећна/ сам.** Srećan /Srećna/ sam
I'm content.	**Задовољан /Задовољна/ сам.** Zadovoljan /Zadovoljna/ sam
I'm in love.	**Заљубљен /Заљубљена/ сам.** Zaljubljen /Zaljubljena/ sam
I'm calm.	**Миран /Мирна/ сам.** Miran /Mirna/ sam
I'm bored.	**Досадно ми је.** Dosadno mi je
I'm tired.	**Уморан /Уморна/ сам.** Umoran /Umorna/ sam
I'm sad.	**Тужан /Тужна/ сам.** Tužan /Tužna/ sam
I'm frightened.	**Уплашен /Уплашена/ сам.** Uplašen /Uplašena/ sam
I'm angry.	**Љут /Љута/ сам.** Ljut /Ljuta/ sam
I'm worried.	**Забринут /Забринута/ сам.** Zabrinut /Zabrinuta/ sam
I'm nervous.	**Нервозан /Нервозна/ сам.** Nervozan /Nervozna/ sam

I'm jealous. (envious)

Љубоморан /Љубоморна/ сам.
Ljubomoran /Ljubomorna/ sam

I'm surprised.

Изненађен /Изненађена/ сам.
Iznenađen /Iznenađena/ sam

I'm perplexed.

Збуњен /Збуњена/ сам.
Zbunjen /Zbunjena/ sam

Problems. Accidents

I've got a problem.	**Имам проблем.** Imam problem
We've got a problem.	**Имамо проблем.** Imamo problem
I'm lost.	**Изгубио /Изгубила/ сам се.** Izgubio /Izgubila/ sam se
I missed the last bus (train).	**Пропустио /пропустила/ сам последњи аутобус (воз).** Propustio /propustila/ sam poslednji autobus (voz)
I don't have any money left.	**Немам више новца.** Nemam više novca
I've lost my ...	**Изгубио /Изгубила/ сам ...** Izgubio /Izgubila/ sam ...
Someone stole my ...	**Неко ми је украо ...** Neko mi je ukrao ...
passport	**пасош** pasoš
wallet	**новчаник** novčanik
papers	**папире** papire
ticket	**карту** kartu
money	**новац** novac
handbag	**ташну** tašnu
camera	**фото-апарат** foto-aparat
laptop	**лаптоп** laptop
tablet computer	**таблет рачунар** tablet računar
mobile phone	**мобилни телефон** mobilni telefon
Help me!	**Помозите ми!** Pomozite mi!
What's happened?	**Шта се десило?** Šta se desilo?

fire	**пожар** požar
shooting	**пуцњава** pucnjava
murder	**убиство** ubistvo
explosion	**експлозија** eksplozija
fight	**туча** tuča

Call the police!	**Позовите полицију!** Pozovite policiju!
Please hurry up!	**Молим вас, пожурите!** Molim vas, požurite!
I'm looking for the police station.	**Тражим полицијску станицу.** Tražim policijsku stanicu
I need to make a call.	**Морам да телефонирам.** Moram da telefoniram
May I use your phone?	**Могу ли да се послужим вашим телефоном?** Mogu li da se poslužim vašim telefonom?

I've been …	**Неко ме је …** Neko me je …
mugged	**покрао** pokrao
robbed	**опљачкао** opljačkao
raped	**силовао** silovao
attacked (beaten up)	**напао** napao

Are you all right?	**Да ли сте добро?** Da li ste dobro?
Did you see who it was?	**Да ли сте видели ко је то био?** Da li ste videli ko je to bio?
Would you be able to recognize the person?	**Да ли бисте могли да препознате ту особу?** Da li biste mogli da prepoznate tu osobu?
Are you sure?	**Да ли сте сигурни?** Da li ste sigurni?

Please calm down.	**Молим вас, смирите се.** Molim vas, smirite se
Take it easy!	**Само полако!** Samo polako!
Don't worry!	**Не брините!** Ne brinite!

Everything will be fine. **Све ће бити у реду.**
Sve će biti u redu

Everything's all right. **Све је у реду.**
Sve je u redu

Come here, please. **Дођите, молим вас.**
Dođite, molim vas

I have some questions for you. **Имам питања за вас.**
Imam pitanja za vas

Wait a moment, please. **Сачекајте, молим вас.**
Sačekajte, molim vas

Do you have any I.D.? **Имате ли исправе?**
Imate li isprave?

Thanks. You can leave now. **Хвала. Можете ићи.**
Hvala. Možete ići

Hands behind your head! **Руке иза главе!**
Ruke iza glave!

You're under arrest! **Ухапшени сте!**
Uhapšeni ste!

Health problems

Please help me.	**Молим вас, помозите ми.** Molim vas, pomozite mi
I don't feel well.	**Не осећам се добро.** Ne osećam se dobro
My husband doesn't feel well.	**Мој муж се не осећа добро.** Moj muž se ne oseća dobro
My son ...	**Мој син ...** Moj sin ...
My father ...	**Мој отац ...** Moj otac ...
My wife doesn't feel well.	**Моја жена се не осећа добро.** Moja žena se ne oseća dobro
My daughter ...	**Моја ћерка ...** Moja ćerka ...
My mother ...	**Моја мајка ...** Moja majka ...
I've got a ...	**Боли ме ...** Boli me ...
headache	**глава** glava
sore throat	**грло** grlo
stomach ache	**стомак** stomak
toothache	**зуб** zub
I feel dizzy.	**Врти ми се у глави.** Vrti mi se u glavi
He has a fever.	**Он има температуру.** On ima temperaturu
She has a fever.	**Она има температуру.** Ona ima temperaturu
I can't breathe.	**Не могу да дишем.** Ne mogu da dišem
I'm short of breath.	**Не могу да удахнем.** Ne mogu da udahnem
I am asthmatic.	**Ја сам асматичар /асматичарка/.** Ja sam asmatičar /asmatičarka/
I am diabetic.	**Ја сам дијабетичар /дијабетичарка/.** Ja sam dijabetičar /dijabetičarka/

I can't sleep.	**Не могу да спавам.** Ne mogu da spavam
food poisoning	**тровање храном** trovanje hranom

It hurts here.	**Овде ме боли.** Ovde me boli
Help me!	**Помозите ми!** Pomozite mi!
I am here!	**Овде сам!** Ovde sam!
We are here!	**Овде смо!** Ovde smo!
Get me out of here!	**Вадите ме одавде!** Vadite me odavde!
I need a doctor.	**Потребан ми је лекар.** Potreban mi je lekar
I can't move.	**Не могу да се померим.** Ne mogu da se pomerim
I can't move my legs.	**Не могу да померам ноге.** Ne mogu da pomeram noge

I have a wound.	**Имам рану.** Imam ranu
Is it serious?	**Да ли је озбиљно?** Da li je ozbiljno?
My documents are in my pocket.	**Документа су ми у џепу.** Dokumenta su mi u džepu
Calm down!	**Смирите се!** Smirite se!
May I use your phone?	**Могу ли да се послужим вашим телефоном?** Mogu li da se poslužim vašim telefonom?

Call an ambulance!	**Позовите хитну помоћ!** Pozovite hitnu pomoć!
It's urgent!	**Хитно је!** Hitno je!
It's an emergency!	**Хитан случај!** Hitan slučaj!
Please hurry up!	**Молим вас, пожурите!** Molim vas, požurite!
Would you please call a doctor?	**Молим вас, зовите доктора?** Molim vas, zovite doktora?
Where is the hospital?	**Где је болница?** Gde je bolnica?

How are you feeling?	**Како се осећате?** Kako se osećate?
Are you all right?	**Да ли сте добро?** Da li ste dobro?

What's happened?

Шта се десило?
Šta se desilo?

I feel better now.

Сада се осећам боље.
Sada se osećam bolje

It's OK.

OK је.
OK je

It's all right.

У реду је.
U redu je

What's happened?	**Шта се десило?** Šta se desilo?
I feel better now.	**Сада се осећам боље.** Sada se osećam bolje
It's OK.	**OK je.** OK je
It's all right.	**У реду је.** U redu je

At the pharmacy

pharmacy (drugstore)	**апотека** apoteka
24-hour pharmacy	**дежурна апотека** dežurna apoteka
Where is the closest pharmacy?	**Где је најближа апотека?** Gde je najbliža apoteka?

Is it open now?	**Да ли је отворена сада?** Da li je otvorena sada?
At what time does it open?	**Када се отвара?** Kada se otvara?
At what time does it close?	**Када се затвара?** Kada se zatvara?

Is it far?	**Да ли је далеко?** Da li je daleko?
Can I get there on foot?	**Могу ли до тамо пешке?** Mogu li do tamo peške?
Can you show me on the map?	**Можете ли да ми покажете на мапи?** Možete li da mi pokažete na mapi?

Please give me something for …	**Молим вас, дајте ми нешто за …** Molim vas, dajte mi nešto za …
a headache	**главобољу** glavobolju
a cough	**кашаљ** kašalj
a cold	**прехладу** prehladu
the flu	**грип** grip

a fever	**температуру** temperaturu
a stomach ache	**стомачне тегобе** stomačne tegobe
nausea	**мучнину** mučninu
diarrhea	**дијареју** dijareju
constipation	**констипацију** konstipaciju
pain in the back	**болове у леђима** bolove u leđima

chest pain	**болове у грудима**
	bolove u grudima
side stitch	**бол у боку**
	bol u boku
abdominal pain	**бол у стомаку**
	bol u stomaku

pill	**пилула**
	pilula
ointment, cream	**маст, крема**
	mast, krema
syrup	**сируп**
	sirup
spray	**спреј**
	sprej
drops	**капи**
	kapi

You need to go to the hospital.	**Морате у болницу.**
	Morate u bolnicu
health insurance	**здравствено осигурање**
	zdravstveno osiguranje
prescription	**рецепт**
	recept
insect repellant	**нешто против инсеката**
	nešto protiv insekata
Band Aid	**фластер**
	flaster

The bare minimum

Excuse me, ...	**Извините, ...** Izvinite, ...
Hello.	**Добар дан.** Dobar dan
Thank you.	**Хвала вам.** Hvala vam
Good bye.	**Довиђења.** Doviđenja
Yes.	**Да.** Da
No.	**Не.** Ne
I don't know.	**Не знам.** Ne znam
Where? | Where to? | When?	**Где? | Куда? | Када?** Gde? | Kuda? | Kada?
I need ...	**Треба ми ...** Treba mi ...
I want ...	**Хоћу ...** Hoću ...
Do you have ...?	**Имате ли ...?** Imate li ...?
Is there a ... here?	**Да ли овде постоји ...?** Da li ovde postoji ...?
May I ...?	**Смем ли ...?** Smem li ...?
..., please (polite request)	**молим** molim
I'm looking for ...	**Тражим ...** Tražim ...
restroom	**тоалет** toalet
ATM	**банкомат** bankomat
pharmacy (drugstore)	**апотеку** apoteku
hospital	**болницу** bolnicu
police station	**полицијску станицу** policijsku stanicu
subway	**метро** metro

taxi	**такси** taksi
train station	**железничку станицу** železničku stanicu

My name is ...	**Ja се зовем ...** Ja se zovem ...
What's your name?	**Како се ви зовете?** Kako se vi zovete?
Could you please help me?	**Да ли бисте, молим вас, могли да ми помогнете?** Da li biste, molim vas, mogli da mi pomognete?
I've got a problem.	**Имам проблем.** Imam problem
I don't feel well.	**Не осећам се добро.** Ne osećam se dobro
Call an ambulance!	**Позовите хитну помоћ!** Pozovite hitnu pomoć!
May I make a call?	**Смем ли да телефонирам?** Smem li da telefoniram?

I'm sorry.	**Извините ...** Izvinite ...
You're welcome.	**Нема на чему.** Nema na čemu

I, me	**ja, мене** ja, mene
you (inform.)	**ти** ti
he	**он** on
she	**она** ona
they (masc.)	**они** oni
they (fem.)	**оне** one
we	**ми** mi
you (pl)	**ви** vi
you (sg, form.)	**ви** vi

ENTRANCE	**УЛАЗ** ULAZ
EXIT	**ИЗЛАЗ** IZLAZ
OUT OF ORDER	**НЕ РАДИ** NE RADI

CLOSED	**ЗАТВОРЕНО**
	ZATVORENO
OPEN	**ОТВОРЕНО**
	OTVORENO
FOR WOMEN	**ЗА ЖЕНЕ**
	ZA ŽENE
FOR MEN	**ЗА МУШКАРЦЕ**
	ZA MUŠKARCE

TOPICAL
VOCABULARY

This section contains more
than 3,000 of the most
important words.
The dictionary will provide
invaluable assistance while
traveling abroad, because
frequently individual words
are enough for you to be
understood.
The dictionary includes a
convenient transcription of
each foreign word

T&P Books Publishing

VOCABULARY
CONTENTS

T&P Books Publishing

BASIC CONCEPTS

T&P Books Publishing

1. Pronouns

I, me	**ja**	ja
you	**ти**	ti
he	**он**	on
she	**она**	ona
it	**оно**	ono
we	**ми**	mi
you (to a group)	**ви**	vi
they (masc.)	**они**	oni
they (fem.)	**оне**	one

2. Greetings. Salutations

Hello! (fam.)	**Здраво!**	Zdravo!
Hello! (form.)	**Добар дан!**	Dobar dan!
Good morning!	**Добро јутро!**	Dobro jutro!
Good afternoon!	**Добар дан!**	Dobar dan!
Good evening!	**Добро вече!**	Dobro veče!
to say hello	**поздрављати се**	pozdravljati se
Hi! (hello)	**Здраво!**	Zdravo!
greeting (n)	**поздрав** (м)	pozdrav
to greet (vt)	**поздрављати**	pozdravljati
How are you? (form.)	**Како сте?**	Kako ste?
How are you? (fam.)	**Како си?**	Kako si?
What's new?	**Шта има ново?**	Šta ima novo?
Goodbye! (form.)	**Довиђења!**	Doviđenja!
Bye! (fam.)	**Здраво!**	Zdravo!
See you soon!	**До скорог виђења!**	Do skorog viđenja!
Farewell!	**Збогом!**	Zbogom!
to say goodbye	**опраштати се**	opraštati se
So long!	**Здраво!**	Zdravo!
Thank you!	**Хвала!**	Hvala!
Thank you very much!	**Хвала лепо!**	Hvala lepo!
You're welcome	**Нема на чему**	Nema na čemu
Don't mention it!	**Никакав проблем!**	Nikakav problem!
It was nothing	**Нема на чему**	Nema na čemu
Excuse me! (fam.)	**Извини!**	Izvini!
Excuse me! (form.)	**Извините!**	Izvinite!

to excuse (forgive)	извинити	izviniti
to apologize (vi)	извињавати се	izvinjavati se
My apologies	Извињавам се	Izvinjavam se
I'm sorry!	Опростите!	Oprostite!
to forgive (vt)	опраштати	opraštati
It's okay! (that's all right)	У реду је!	U redu je!
please (adv)	молим	molim

Don't forget!	Немојте да заборавите!	Nemojte da zaboravite!
Certainly!	Свакако!	Svakako!
Of course not!	Наравно да не!	Naravno da ne!
Okay! (I agree)	Цлажем се!	Clažem se!
That's enough!	Доста!	Dosta!

3. Questions

Who?	Ко?	Ko?
What?	Шта?	Šta?
Where? (at, in)	Где?	Gde?
Where (to)?	Куда?	Kuda?
From where?	Одакле?	Odakle?
When?	Када?	Kada?
Why? (What for?)	Зашто? Због чега?	Zašto? Zbog čega?
Why? (~ are you crying?)	Зашто?	Zašto?

What for?	Због чега?	Zbog čega?
How? (in what way)	Како?	Kako?
What? (What kind of ...?)	Какав?	Kakav?
Which?	Који?	Koji?

To whom?	Коме?	Kome?
About whom?	О коме?	O kome?
About what?	О чему?	O čemu?
With whom?	С ким?	S kim?

| How many? How much? | Колико? | Koliko? |
| Whose? | Чији? Чија? Чије? | Čiji? Čija? Čije? |

4. Prepositions

with (accompanied by)	са	sa
without	без	bez
to (indicating direction)	у	u
about (talking ~ ...)	о	o
before (in time)	пре	pre
in front of ...	испред	ispred
under (beneath, below)	испод	ispod
above (over)	изнад	iznad

on (atop)	**на**	na
from (off, out of)	**из**	iz
of (made from)	**од**	od
in (e.g., ~ ten minutes)	**за**	za
over (across the top of)	**преко**	preko

5. Function words. Adverbs. Part 1

Where? (at, in)	**Где?**	Gde?
here (adv)	**овде**	ovde
there (adv)	**тамо**	tamo
somewhere (to be)	**негде**	negde
nowhere (not anywhere)	**нигде**	nigde
by (near, beside)	**код**	kod
by the window	**код прозора**	kod prozora
Where (to)?	**Куда?**	Kuda?
here (e.g., come ~!)	**овамо**	ovamo
there (e.g., to go ~)	**тамо**	tamo
from here (adv)	**одавде**	odavde
from there (adv)	**оданде**	odande
close (adv)	**близу**	blizu
far (adv)	**далеко**	daleko
near (e.g., ~ Paris)	**у близини**	u blizini
nearby (adv)	**у близини**	u blizini
not far (adv)	**недалеко**	nedaleko
left (adj)	**леви**	levi
on the left	**слева**	sleva
to the left	**лево**	levo
right (adj)	**десни**	desni
on the right	**здесна**	zdesna
to the right	**десно**	desno
in front (adv)	**спреда**	spreda
front (as adj)	**предњи**	prednji
ahead (the kids ran ~)	**унапред**	unapred
behind (adv)	**иза**	iza
from behind	**отпозади**	otpozadi
back (towards the rear)	**унатраг**	unatrag
middle	**средина** (ж)	sredina
in the middle	**у средини**	u sredini

at the side	са стране	sa strane
everywhere (adv)	свуда	svuda
around (in all directions)	око	oko

from inside	изнутра	iznutra
somewhere (to go)	некуда	nekuda
straight (directly)	право	pravo
back (e.g., come ~)	назад	nazad

| from anywhere | однекуд | odnekud |
| from somewhere | од негде | od negde |

firstly (adv)	прво	prvo
secondly (adv)	друго	drugo
thirdly (adv)	треће	treće

suddenly (adv)	изненада	iznenada
at first (in the beginning)	у почетку	u početku
for the first time	први пут	prvi put
long before ...	много пре ...	mnogo pre ...
anew (over again)	поново	ponovo
for good (adv)	заувек	zauvek

never (adv)	никад	nikad
again (adv)	опет	opet
now (adv)	сада	sada
often (adv)	често	često
then (adv)	тада	tada
urgently (quickly)	хитно	hitno
usually (adv)	обично	obično

by the way, ...	узгред, ...	uzgred, ...
possible (that is ~)	могуће	moguće
probably (adv)	вероватно	verovatno
maybe (adv)	можда	možda
besides ...	осим тога ...	osim toga ...
that's why ...	због тога ...	zbog toga ...
in spite of ...	без обзира на ...	bez obzira na ...
thanks to ...	захваљујући ...	zahvaljujući ...

what (pron.)	шта	šta
that (conj.)	да	da
something	нешто	nešto
anything (something)	нешто	nešto
nothing	ништа	ništa

who (pron.)	ко	ko
someone	неко	neko
somebody	неко	neko

| nobody | нико | niko |
| nowhere (a voyage to ~) | никуд | nikud |

| nobody's | ничији | ničiji |
| somebody's | нечији | nečiji |

so (I'm ~ glad)	тако	tako
also (as well)	такође	takođe
too (as well)	исто, такође	isto, takođe

6. Function words. Adverbs. Part 2

Why?	Зашто?	Zašto?
for some reason	из неког разлога	iz nekog razloga
because ...	зато што ...	zato što ...
for some purpose	због нечега	zbog nečega

and	и	i
or	или	ili
but	али	ali
for (e.g., ~ me)	за	za

too (~ many people)	сувише, превише	suviše, previše
only (exclusively)	само	samo
exactly (adv)	тачно	tačno
about (more or less)	око	oko

approximately (adv)	приближно	približno
approximate (adj)	приближан	približan
almost (adv)	скоро, замало	skoro, zamalo
the rest	остало (c)	ostalo

the other (second)	други	drugi
other (different)	другачији	drugačiji
each (adj)	свак	svak
any (no matter which)	било који	bilo koji
many, much (a lot of)	много	mnogo
many people	многи	mnogi
all (everyone)	сви	svi

in return for ...	у замену за ...	u zamenu za ...
in exchange (adv)	у замену	u zamenu
by hand (made)	ручно	ručno
hardly (negative opinion)	једва да	jedva da

probably (adv)	вероватно	verovatno
on purpose (intentionally)	намерно	namerno
by accident (adv)	случајно	slučajno

very (adv)	врло	vrlo
for example (adv)	на пример	na primer
between	између	između
among	међу	među

| so much (such a lot) | толико | toliko |
| especially (adv) | нарочито | naročito |

NUMBERS. MISCELLANEOUS

T&P Books Publishing

7. Cardinal numbers. Part 1

0 zero	нула	nula
1 one	један	jedan
2 two	два	dva
3 three	три	tri
4 four	четири	četiri
5 five	пет	pet
6 six	шест	šest
7 seven	седам	sedam
8 eight	осам	osam
9 nine	девет	devet
10 ten	десет	deset
11 eleven	једанаест	jedanaest
12 twelve	дванаест	dvanaest
13 thirteen	тринаест	trinaest
14 fourteen	четрнаест	četrnaest
15 fifteen	петнаест	petnaest
16 sixteen	шеснаест	šesnaest
17 seventeen	седамнаест	sedamnaest
18 eighteen	осамнаест	osamnaest
19 nineteen	деветнаест	devetnaest
20 twenty	двадесет	dvadeset
21 twenty-one	двадесет и један	dvadeset i jedan
22 twenty-two	двадесет и два	dvadeset i dva
23 twenty-three	двадесет и три	dvadeset i tri
30 thirty	тридесет	trideset
31 thirty-one	тридесет и један	trideset i jedan
32 thirty-two	тридесет и два	trideset i dva
33 thirty-three	тридесет и три	trideset i tri
40 forty	четрдесет	četrdeset
41 forty-one	четрдесет и један	četrdeset i jedan
42 forty-two	четрдесет и два	četrdeset i dva
43 forty-three	четрдесет и три	četrdeset i tri
50 fifty	педесет	pedeset
51 fifty-one	педесет и један	pedeset i jedan
52 fifty-two	педесет и два	pedeset i dva
53 fifty-three	педесет и три	pedeset i tri
60 sixty	шездесет	šezdeset

61 sixty-one	шездесет и један	šezdeset i jedan
62 sixty-two	шездесет и два	šezdeset i dva
63 sixty-three	шездесет и три	šezdeset i tri

70 seventy	седамдесет	sedamdeset
71 seventy-one	седамдесет и један	sedamdeset i jedan
72 seventy-two	седамдесет и два	sedamdeset i dva
73 seventy-three	седамдесет и три	sedamdeset i tri

80 eighty	осамдесет	osamdeset
81 eighty-one	осамдесет и један	osamdeset i jedan
82 eighty-two	осамдесет и два	osamdeset i dva
83 eighty-three	осамдесет и три	osamdeset i tri

90 ninety	деведесет	devedeset
91 ninety-one	деведесет и један	devedeset i jedan
92 ninety-two	деведесет и два	devedeset i dva
93 ninety-three	деведесет и три	devedeset i tri

8. Cardinal numbers. Part 2

100 one hundred	сто	sto
200 two hundred	двеста	dvesta
300 three hundred	триста	trista
400 four hundred	четиристо	četiristo
500 five hundred	петсто	petsto

600 six hundred	шестсто	šeststo
700 seven hundred	седамсто	sedamsto
800 eight hundred	осамсто	osamsto
900 nine hundred	деветсто	devetsto

1000 one thousand	хиљада	hiljada
2000 two thousand	две хиљаде	dve hiljade
3000 three thousand	три хиљаде	tri hiljade
10000 ten thousand	десет хиљада	deset hiljada
one hundred thousand	сто хиљада	sto hiljada
million	милион (м)	milion
billion	милијарда (ж)	milijarda

9. Ordinal numbers

first (adj)	први	prvi
second (adj)	други	drugi
third (adj)	трећи	treći
fourth (adj)	четврти	četvrti
fifth (adj)	пети	peti
sixth (adj)	шести	šesti

seventh (adj)	седми	sedmi
eighth (adj)	осми	osmi
ninth (adj)	девети	deveti
tenth (adj)	десети	deseti

COLOURS. UNITS OF MEASUREMENT

T&P Books Publishing

10. Colors

color	боја (ж)	boja
shade (tint)	нијанса (ж)	nijansa
hue	тон (м)	ton
rainbow	дуга (ж)	duga
white (adj)	бео	beo
black (adj)	црн	crn
gray (adj)	сив	siv
green (adj)	зелен	zelen
yellow (adj)	жут	žut
red (adj)	црвен	crven
blue (adj)	плав	plav
light blue (adj)	светло плав	svetlo plav
pink (adj)	ружичаст	ružičast
orange (adj)	наранџаст	narandžast
violet (adj)	љубичаст	ljubičast
brown (adj)	браон	braon
golden (adj)	златан	zlatan
silvery (adj)	сребрни	srebrni
beige (adj)	беж	bež
cream (adj)	крем	krem
turquoise (adj)	тиркизан	tirkizan
cherry red (adj)	боја вишње	boja višnje
lilac (adj)	лила	lila
crimson (adj)	гримизан	grimizan
light (adj)	светао	svetao
dark (adj)	таман	taman
bright, vivid (adj)	јарки	jarki
colored (pencils)	обојен	obojen
color (e.g., ~ film)	у боји	u boji
black-and-white (adj)	црно-бели	crno-beli
plain (one-colored)	једнобојан	jednobojan
multicolored (adj)	разнобојан	raznobojan

11. Units of measurement

weight	тежина (ж)	težina
length	дужина (ж)	dužina

width	ширина (ж)	širina
height	висина (ж)	visina
depth	дубина (ж)	dubina
volume	запремина (ж)	zapremina
area	површина (ж)	površina

gram	грам (м)	gram
milligram	милиграм (м)	miligram
kilogram	килограм (м)	kilogram
ton	тона (ж)	tona
pound	фунта (ж)	funta
ounce	унца (ж)	unca

meter	метар (м)	metar
millimeter	милиметар (м)	milimetar
centimeter	сантиметар (м)	santimetar
kilometer	километар (м)	kilometar
mile	миља (ж)	milja

inch	палац (м)	palac
foot	стопа (ж)	stopa
yard	јарда (ж)	jarda

square meter	квадратни метар (м)	kvadratni metar
hectare	хектар (м)	hektar
liter	литар (м)	litar
degree	степен (ж)	stepen
volt	волт (м)	volt
ampere	ампер (м)	amper
horsepower	коњска снага (ж)	konjska snaga

quantity	количина (ж)	količina
a little bit of ...	мало ...	malo ...
half	половина (ж)	polovina
dozen	туце (с)	tuce
piece (item)	комад (м)	komad

| size | величина (ж) | veličina |
| scale (map ~) | размер (м) | razmer |

minimal (adj)	минималан	minimalan
the smallest (adj)	најмањи	najmanji
medium (adj)	средњи	srednji
maximal (adj)	максималан	maksimalan
the largest (adj)	највећи	najveći

12. Containers

| canning jar (glass ~) | тегла (ж) | tegla |
| can | лименка (ж) | limenka |

| bucket | **ведро** (с) | vedro |
| barrel | **буре** (с) | bure |

wash basin (e.g., plastic ~)	**лавор** (м)	lavor
tank (100L water ~)	**резервоар** (м)	rezervoar
hip flask	**чутурица** (ж)	čuturica
jerrycan	**канта** (ж)	kanta
tank (e.g., tank car)	**цистерна** (ж)	cisterna

mug	**кригла** (ж)	krigla
cup (of coffee, etc.)	**шоља** (ж)	šolja
saucer	**тацна** (ж)	tacna
glass (tumbler)	**чаша** (ж)	čaša
wine glass	**чаша** (ж) **за вино**	čaša za vino
stock pot (soup pot)	**лонац** (м)	lonac

| bottle (~ of wine) | **боца** (ж), **флаша** (ж) | boca, flaša |
| neck (of the bottle, etc.) | **грлић** (м) | grlić |

carafe (decanter)	**бокал** (м)	bokal
pitcher	**крчаг** (м)	krčag
vessel (container)	**суд** (м)	sud
pot (crock, stoneware ~)	**лонац** (м)	lonac
vase	**ваза** (ж)	vaza

bottle (perfume ~)	**боца, бочица** (ж)	boca, bočica
vial, small bottle	**бочица** (ж)	bočica
tube (of toothpaste)	**туба** (ж)	tuba

sack (bag)	**џак** (м)	džak
bag (paper ~, plastic ~)	**кеса** (ж)	kesa
pack (of cigarettes, etc.)	**пакла** (ж)	pakla

box (e.g., shoebox)	**кутија** (ж)	kutija
crate	**сандук** (м)	sanduk
basket	**корпа** (ж)	korpa

MAIN VERBS

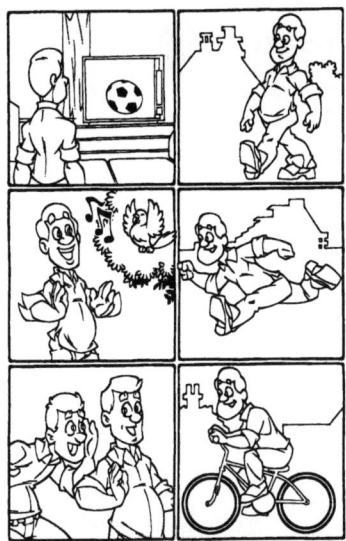

T&P Books Publishing

to advise (vt)	саветовати	savetovati
to agree (say yes)	слагати се	slagati se
to answer (vi, vt)	одговарати	odgovarati
to apologize (vi)	извињавати се	izvinjavati se
to arrive (vi)	долазити	dolaziti
to ask (~ oneself)	питати	pitati
to ask (~ sb to do sth)	молити	moliti
to be (vi)	бити	biti
to be afraid	плашити се, бојати се	plašiti se, bojati se
to be hungry	бити гладан	biti gladan
to be interested in ...	интересовати се	interesovati se
to be needed	бити потребан	biti potreban
to be surprised	бити изненађен	biti iznenađen
to be thirsty	бити жедан	biti žedan
to begin (vt)	почињати	počinjati
to belong to ...	припадати	pripadati
to boast (vi)	хвалисати се	hvalisati se
to break (split into pieces)	ломити	lomiti
to call (~ for help)	звати	zvati
can (v aux)	моћи	moći
to catch (vt)	хватати	hvatati
to change (vt)	променити	promeniti
to choose (select)	бирати	birati
to come down (the stairs)	спуштати се	spuštati se
to compare (vt)	упоређивати	upoređivati
to complain (vi, vt)	жалити се	žaliti se
to confuse (mix up)	бркати	brkati
to continue (vt)	наставити	nastaviti
to control (vt)	контролисати	kontrolisati
to cook (dinner)	кувати	kuvati
to cost (vt)	коштати	koštati
to count (add up)	сабирати	sabirati
to count on ...	рачунати на ...	računati na ...
to create (vt)	направити	napraviti
to cry (weep)	плакати	plakati

14. The most important verbs. Part 2

to deceive (vi, vt)	обманути	obmanuti
to decorate (tree, street)	украшавати	ukrašavati
to defend (a country, etc.)	бранити	braniti
to demand (request firmly)	захтевати, тражити	zahtevati, tražiti
to dig (vt)	копати	kopati

to discuss (vt)	расправљати	raspravljati
to do (vt)	радити	raditi
to doubt (have doubts)	сумњати	sumnjati
to drop (let fall)	испустити	ispustiti
to enter (room, house, etc.)	ући	ući

to excuse (forgive)	опростити	oprostiti
to exist (vi)	постојати	postojati
to expect (foresee)	предвидети	predvideti

to explain (vt)	објашњавати	objašnjavati
to fall (vi)	падати	padati

to find (vt)	наћи	naći
to finish (vt)	завршавати	završavati
to fly (vi)	летети	leteti

to follow ... (come after)	пратити	pratiti
to forget (vi, vt)	заборављати	zaboravljati

to forgive (vt)	опраштати	opraštati
to give (vt)	давати	davati

to give a hint	наговестити	nagovestiti
to go (on foot)	ићи	ići

to go for a swim	купати се	kupati se
to go out (for dinner, etc.)	изаћи	izaći
to guess (the answer)	одгонетнути	odgonetnuti

to have (vt)	имати	imati
to have breakfast	доручковати	doručkovati
to have dinner	вечерати	večerati

to have lunch	ручати	ručati
to hear (vt)	чути	čuti

to help (vt)	помагати	pomagati
to hide (vt)	крити	kriti
to hope (vi, vt)	надати се	nadati se
to hunt (vi, vt)	ловити	loviti
to hurry (vi)	журити се	žuriti se

15. The most important verbs. Part 3

to inform (vt)	информисати	informisati
to insist (vi, vt)	инсистирати	insistirati
to insult (vt)	вређати	vređati
to invite (vt)	позвати	pozvati
to joke (vi)	шалити се	šaliti se
to keep (vt)	чувати	čuvati
to keep silent	ћутати	ćutati
to kill (vt)	убити	ubiti
to know (sb)	знати	znati
to know (sth)	знати	znati
to laugh (vi)	смејати се	smejati se
to liberate (city, etc.)	ослободити	osloboditi
to like (I like …)	свиђати се	sviđati se
to look for … (search)	тражити	tražiti
to love (sb)	волети	voleti
to make a mistake	грешити	grešiti
to manage, to run	руководити	rukovoditi
to mean (signify)	означавати	označavati
to mention (talk about)	спомињати	spominjati
to miss (school, etc.)	пропустити	propustiti
to notice (see)	запазити	zapaziti
to object (vi, vt)	приговарати	prigovarati
to observe (see)	посматрати, гледати	posmatrati, gledati
to open (vt)	отворити	otvoriti
to order (meal, etc.)	наручити	naručiti
to order (mil.)	наређивати	naređivati
to own (possess)	поседовати	posedovati
to participate (vi)	учествовати	učestvovati
to pay (vi, vt)	платити	platiti
to permit (vt)	дозвољавати	dozvoljavati
to plan (vt)	планирати	planirati
to play (children)	играти се	igrati se
to pray (vi, vt)	молити се	moliti se
to prefer (vt)	давати предност	davati prednost
to promise (vt)	обећати	obećati
to pronounce (vt)	изговарати	izgovarati
to propose (vt)	предлагати	predlagati
to punish (vt)	казнити	kazniti

16. The most important verbs. Part 4

to read (vi, vt)	читати	čitati
to recommend (vt)	препоручивати	preporučivati

to refuse (vi, vt)	одбити	odbiti
to regret (be sorry)	жалити	žaliti
to rent (sth from sb)	изнајмити	iznajmiti

to repeat (say again)	поновити	ponoviti
to reserve, to book	резервисати	rezervisati
to run (vi)	трчати	trčati
to save (rescue)	спасити	spasiti
to say (~ thank you)	рећи	reći

to scold (vt)	грдити	grditi
to see (vt)	видети	videti
to sell (vt)	продавати	prodavati
to send (vt)	послати	poslati
to shoot (vi)	пуцати	pucati

to shout (vi)	викати	vikati
to show (vt)	показати	pokazati
to sign (document)	потписати	potpisati
to sit down (vi)	сести	sesti

to smile (vi)	осмехнути се	osmehnuti se
to speak (vi, vt)	говорити	govoriti
to steal (money, etc.)	красти	krasti
to stop (for pause, etc.)	зауставити се	zaustaviti se
to stop (please ~ calling me)	прекинути	prekinuti

to study (vt)	студирати	studirati
to swim (vi)	пливати	plivati
to take (vt)	узети	uzeti
to think (vi, vt)	мислити	misliti
to threaten (vt)	претити	pretiti

to touch (with hands)	дирати	dirati
to translate (vt)	преводити	prevoditi
to trust (vt)	веровати	verovati
to try (attempt)	пробати	probati
to turn (e.g., ~ left)	скренути	skrenuti

to underestimate (vt)	потцењивати	potcenjivati
to understand (vt)	разумети	razumeti
to unite (vt)	ујединити	ujediniti
to wait (vt)	чекати	čekati

to want (wish, desire)	хтети	hteti
to warn (vt)	упозорити	upozoriti
to work (vi)	радити	raditi
to write (vt)	писати	pisati
to write down	записивати	zapisivati

TIME. CALENDAR

T&P Books Publishing

17. Weekdays

Monday	понедељак (м)	ponedeljak
Tuesday	уторак (м)	utorak
Wednesday	среда (ж)	sreda
Thursday	четвртак (м)	četvrtak
Friday	петак (м)	petak
Saturday	субота (ж)	subota
Sunday	недеља (ж)	nedelja
today (adv)	данас	danas
tomorrow (adv)	сутра	sutra
the day after tomorrow	прекосутра	prekosutra
yesterday (adv)	јуче	juče
the day before yesterday	прекјуче	prekjuče
day	дан (м)	dan
working day	радни дан (м)	radni dan
public holiday	празничан дан (м)	prazničan dan
day off	слободан дан (м)	slobodan dan
weekend	викенд (м)	vikend
all day long	цео дан	ceo dan
the next day (adv)	сутрадан	sutradan
two days ago	пре два дана	pre dva dana
the day before	уочи	uoči
daily (adj)	свакодневни	svakodnevni
every day (adv)	сваки дан	svaki dan
week	недеља (ж)	nedelja
last week (adv)	прошле недеље	prošle nedelje
next week (adv)	следеће недеље	sledeće nedelje
weekly (adj)	недељни	nedeljni
every week (adv)	недељно	nedeljno
twice a week	два пута недељно	dva puta nedeljno
every Tuesday	сваког уторка	svakog utorka

18. Hours. Day and night

morning	јутро (с)	jutro
in the morning	ујутру	ujutru
noon, midday	подне (с)	podne
in the afternoon	поподне	popodne
evening	вече (с)	veče

in the evening	увече	uveče
night	ноћ (ж)	noć
at night	ноћу	noću
midnight	поноћ (ж)	ponoć

second	секунд (м)	sekund
minute	минут (м)	minut
hour	сат (м)	sat
half an hour	пола (ж) сата	pola sata
a quarter-hour	четврт сата (ж)	četvrt sata
fifteen minutes	петнаест минута	petnaest minuta
24 hours	двадесет четири сата	dvadeset četiri sata

sunrise	излазак (м) сунца	izlazak sunca
dawn	свануће (с)	svanuće
early morning	рано јутро (с)	rano jutro
sunset	залазак (м) сунца	zalazak sunca

early in the morning	рано ујутру	rano ujutru
this morning	јутрос	jutros
tomorrow morning	сутра ујутру	sutra ujutru

this afternoon	овог поподнева	ovog popodneva
in the afternoon	поподне	popodne
tomorrow afternoon	сутра поподне	sutra popodne

| tonight (this evening) | вечерас | večeras |
| tomorrow night | сутра увече | sutra uveče |

at 3 o'clock sharp	тачно у три сата	tačno u tri sata
about 4 o'clock	око четири сата	oko četiri sata
by 12 o'clock	до дванаест сати	do dvanaest sati

in 20 minutes	за двадесет минута	za dvadeset minuta
in an hour	за сат времена	za sat vremena
on time (adv)	на време	na vreme

a quarter of …	четврт (м)	četvrt
within an hour	у року од сат времена	u roku od sat vremena
every 15 minutes	сваких петнаест минута	svakih petnaest minuta
round the clock	цео дан и ноћ	ceo dan i noć

19. Months. Seasons

January	јануар (м)	januar
February	фебруар (м)	februar
March	март (м)	mart
April	април (м)	april
May	мај (м)	maj
June	јун (м), јуни (м)	jun, juni

July	јули (м)	juli
August	август (м)	avgust
September	септембар (м)	septembar
October	октобар (м)	oktobar
November	новембар (м)	novembar
December	децембар (м)	decembar

spring	пролеће (с)	proleće
in spring	у пролеће	u proleće
spring (as adj)	пролећни	prolećni

summer	лето (с)	leto
in summer	лети	leti
summer (as adj)	летњи	letnji

fall	јесен (ж)	jesen
in fall	у јесен	u jesen
fall (as adj)	јесењи	jesenji

winter	зима (ж)	zima
in winter	зими	zimi
winter (as adj)	зимски	zimski

month	месец (м)	mesec
this month	овог месеца	ovog meseca
next month	следећег месеца	sledećeg meseca
last month	прошлог месеца	prošlog meseca

a month ago	пре месец дана	pre mesec dana
in a month (a month later)	за месец дана	za mesec dana
in 2 months (2 months later)	за два месеца	za dva meseca
the whole month	цео месец	ceo mesec
all month long	током целог месеца	tokom celog meseca

monthly (~ magazine)	месечни	mesečni
monthly (adv)	месечно	mesečno
every month	сваког месеца	svakog meseca
twice a month	два пута месечно	dva puta mesečno

year	година (ж)	godina
this year	ове године	ove godine
next year	следеће године	sledeće godine
last year	прошла година	prošla godina

a year ago	пре годину дана	pre godinu dana
in a year	за годину дана	za godinu dana
in two years	за две године	za dve godine
the whole year	цела година	cela godina
all year long	током целе године	tokom cele godine
every year	сваке године	svake godine
annual (adj)	годишњи	godišnji

annually (adv)	годишње	godišnje
4 times a year	четири пута годишње	četiri puta godišnje

date (e.g., today's ~)	датум (м)	datum
date (e.g., ~ of birth)	датум (м)	datum
calendar	календар (м)	kalendar

half a year	пола (ж) године	pola godine
six months	полугодиште (с)	polugodište
season (summer, etc.)	сезона (ж)	sezona
century	век (м)	vek

TRAVEL. HOTEL

T&P Books Publishing

20. Trip. Travel

tourism, travel	туризам (м)	turizam
tourist	туриста (м)	turista
trip, voyage	путовање (с)	putovanje
adventure	авантура (ж)	avantura
trip, journey	путовање (с)	putovanje
vacation	годишњи одмор (м)	godišnji odmor
to be on vacation	бити на годишњем одмору	biti na godišnjem odmoru
rest	одмор (м)	odmor
train	воз (м)	voz
by train	возом	vozom
airplane	авион (м)	avion
by airplane	авионом	avionom
by car	колима	kolima
by ship	бродом	brodom
luggage	пртљаг (м)	prtljag
suitcase	кофер (м)	kofer
luggage cart	колица (ж) за пртљаг	kolica za prtljag
passport	пасош (м)	pasoš
visa	виза (ж)	viza
ticket	карта (ж)	karta
air ticket	авионска карта (ж)	avionska karta
guidebook	водич (м)	vodič
map (tourist ~)	мапа (ж)	mapa
area (rural ~)	подручје (с)	područje
place, site	место (с)	mesto
exotica (n)	егзотика (ж)	egzotika
exotic (adj)	егзотичан	egzotičan
amazing (adj)	диван	divan
group	група (ж)	grupa
excursion, sightseeing tour	екскурзија (ж)	ekskurzija
guide (person)	водич (м)	vodič

21. Hotel

hotel	гостионица (ж)	gostionica
hotel	хотел (м)	hotel

motel	мотел (м)	motel
three-star (~ hotel)	три звездице	tri zvezdice
five-star	пет звездица	pet zvezdica
to stay (in a hotel, etc.)	одсести	odsesti

room	соба (ж)	soba
single room	једнокреветна соба (ж)	jednokrevetna soba
double room	двокреветна соба (ж)	dvokrevetna soba
to book a room	резервисати собу	rezervisati sobu

| half board | полупансион (м) | polupansion |
| full board | пун пансион (м) | pun pansion |

with bath	са купатилом	sa kupatilom
with shower	са тушем	sa tušem
satellite television	сателитска телевизија (ж)	satelitska televizija
air-conditioner	клима (ж)	klima
towel	пешкир (м)	peškir
key	кључ (м)	ključ

administrator	администратор (м)	administrator
chambermaid	собарица (ж)	sobarica
porter, bellboy	носач (м)	nosač
doorman	портир (м)	portir

restaurant	ресторан (м)	restoran
pub, bar	бар (м)	bar
breakfast	доручак (м)	doručak
dinner	вечера (ж)	večera
buffet	шведски сто (м)	švedski sto

| lobby | фоаје (м) | foaje |
| elevator | лифт (м) | lift |

| DO NOT DISTURB | НЕ УЗНЕМИРАВАТИ | NE UZNEMIRAVATI |
| NO SMOKING | ЗАБРАЊЕНО ПУШЕЊЕ | ZABRANJENO PUŠENJE |

22. Sightseeing

monument	споменик (м)	spomenik
fortress	тврђава (ж)	tvrđava
palace	палата (ж), дворац (м)	palata, dvorac
castle	замак (м)	zamak
tower	кула (ж)	kula
mausoleum	маузолеј (м)	mauzolej

architecture	архитектура (ж)	arhitektura
medieval (adj)	средњовекован	srednjovekovan
ancient (adj)	старински	starinski

| national (adj) | народан | narodan |
| famous (monument, etc.) | чувен | čuven |

tourist	туриста (м)	turista
guide (person)	водич (м)	vodič
excursion, sightseeing tour	екскурзија (ж)	ekskurzija
to show (vt)	показивати	pokazivati
to tell (vt)	рећи	reći

to find (vt)	наћи	naći
to get lost (lose one's way)	изгубити се	izgubiti se
map (e.g., subway ~)	мапа (ж)	mapa
map (e.g., city ~)	мапа (ж)	mapa

| souvenir, gift | сувенир (м) | suvenir |
| gift shop | продавница (ж) сувенира | prodavnica suvenira |

| to take pictures | сликати | slikati |
| to have one's picture taken | сликати се | slikati se |

TRANSPORTATION

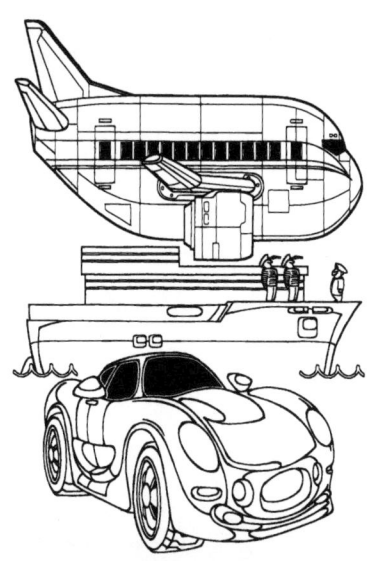

T&P Books Publishing

airport	**аеродром** (м)	aerodrom
airplane	**авион** (м)	avion
airline	**авио-компанија** (ж)	avio-kompanija
air traffic controller	**контролор** (м) **лета**	kontrolor leta
departure	**полазак** (м)	polazak
arrival	**долазак** (м)	dolazak
to arrive (by plane)	**долетети**	doleteti
departure time	**време** (с) **поласка**	vreme polaska
arrival time	**време** (с) **доласка**	vreme dolaska
to be delayed	**каснити**	kasniti
flight delay	**кашњење** (с) **лета**	kašnjenje leta
information board	**информативна табла** (ж)	informativna tabla
information	**информација** (ж)	informacija
to announce (vt)	**објавити**	objaviti
flight (e.g., next ~)	**лет** (м)	let
customs	**царина** (ж)	carina
customs officer	**цариник** (м)	carinar
customs declaration	**царинска декларација** (ж)	carinska deklaracija
to fill out (vt)	**попунити**	popuniti
to fill out the declaration	**попунити декларацију**	popuniti deklaraciju
passport control	**пасошна контрола** (ж)	pasošna kontrola
luggage	**пртљаг** (м)	prtljag
hand luggage	**ручни пртљаг** (м)	ručni prtljag
luggage cart	**колица** (ж) **за пртљаг**	kolica za prtljag
landing	**слетање** (с)	sletanje
landing strip	**писта** (ж) **за слетање**	pista za sletanje
to land (vi)	**спуштати се**	spuštati se
airstairs	**степенице** (ж мн)	stepenice
check-in	**пријављивање, чекирање** (с)	prijavljivanje, čekiranje
check-in counter	**шалтер** (м) **за чекирање**	šalter za čekiranje
to check-in (vi)	**пријавити се, чекирати се**	prijaviti se, čekirati se
boarding pass	**бординг карта** (ж)	bording karta

departure gate	излаз (м) за укрцавање	izlaz za ukrcavanje
transit	транзит (м)	tranzit
to wait (vt)	чекати	čekati
departure lounge	чекаоница (ж)	čekaonica
to see off	испраћати	ispraćati
to say goodbye	опраштати се	opraštati se

24. Airplane

airplane	авион (м)	avion
air ticket	авионска карта (ж)	avionska karta
airline	авио-компанија (ж)	avio-kompanija
airport	аеродром (м)	aerodrom
supersonic (adj)	суперсоничан	supersoničan

captain	командир (м)	komandir
crew	посада (ж)	posada
pilot	пилот (м)	pilot
flight attendant (fem.)	стјуардеса (ж)	stjuardesa
navigator	навигатор (м)	navigator

wings	крила (с мн)	krila
tail	реп (м)	rep
cockpit	кабина (ж)	kabina
engine	мотор (м)	motor
undercarriage (landing gear)	шасија (ж)	šasija
turbine	турбина (ж)	turbina

propeller	пропелер (м)	propeler
black box	црна кутија (ж)	crna kutija
yoke (control column)	управљач (м)	upravljač
fuel	гориво (с)	gorivo

safety card	упутство (с) за безбедност	uputstvo za bezbednost
oxygen mask	маска (ж) за кисеоник	maska za kiseonik
uniform	униформа (ж)	uniforma
life vest	прслук (м) за спасавање	prsluk za spasavanje
parachute	падобран (м)	padobran

takeoff	полетање (с)	poletanje
to take off (vi)	полетети	poleteti
runway	писта (ж)	pista

visibility	видљивост (ж)	vidljivost
flight (act of flying)	лет (м)	let
altitude	висина (ж)	visina
air pocket	ваздушни џеп (м)	vazdušni džep
seat	седиште (с)	sedište

headphones	слушалице (ж мн)	slušalice
folding tray (tray table)	сточић (м) на расклапање	stočić na rasklapanje
airplane window	прозор (м)	prozor
aisle	пролаз (м)	prolaz

25. Train

train	воз (м)	voz
commuter train	електрични воз (м)	električni voz
express train	брзи воз (м)	brzi voz
diesel locomotive	дизел локомотива (ж)	dizel lokomotiva
steam locomotive	парна локомотива (ж)	parna lokomotiva

| passenger car | вагон (м) | vagon |
| dining car | кола (ж) за ручавање | kola za ručavanje |

rails	шине (ж мн)	šine
railroad	железница (ж)	železnica
railway tie	праг (м)	prag

platform (railway ~)	перон (м)	peron
track (~ 1, 2, etc.)	колосек (м)	kolosek
semaphore	семафор (м)	semafor
station	станица (ж)	stanica

engineer (train driver)	машиновођа (м)	mašinovođa
porter (of luggage)	носач (м)	nosač
car attendant	послужитељ (м) у возу	poslužitelj u vozu
passenger	путник (м)	putnik
conductor (ticket inspector)	контролор (м)	kontrolor

| corridor (in train) | ходник (м) | hodnik |
| emergency brake | кочница (ж) за случај опасности | kočnica za slučaj opasnosti |

compartment	кабина (ж)	kabina
berth	лежај (м)	ležaj
upper berth	горњи лежај (м)	gornji ležaj
lower berth	доњи лежај (м)	donji ležaj
bed linen, bedding	постељина (ж)	posteljina

ticket	карта (ж)	karta
schedule	ред (м) вожње	red vožnje
information display	табла (ж) за информације	tabla za informacije

| to leave, to depart | одлазити | odlaziti |
| departure (of train) | полазак (м) | polazak |

| to arrive (ab. train) | долазити | dolaziti |
| arrival | долазак (м) | dolazak |

to arrive by train	стићи возом	stići vozom
to get on the train	сести у воз	sesti u voz
to get off the train	сићи с воза	sići s voza

train wreck	железничка несрећа (ж)	železnička nesreća
to derail (vi)	исклизнути из шина	iskliznuti iz šina
steam locomotive	парна локомотива (ж)	parna lokomotiva
stoker, fireman	ложач (м)	ložač
firebox	ложиште (с)	ložište
coal	угаљ (м)	ugalj

26. Ship

| ship | брод (м) | brod |
| vessel | пловило (с) | plovilo |

steamship	пароброд (м)	parobrod
riverboat	речни чамац (м)	rečni čamac
cruise ship	брод (м) за крстарење	brod za krstarenje
cruiser	крстарица (ж)	krstarica

yacht	јахта (ж)	jahta
tugboat	тегљач (м)	tegljač
barge	шлеп (м)	šlep
ferry	трајект (м)	trajekt

| sailing ship | једрењак (м) | jedrenjak |
| brigantine | бригантина (ж) | brigantina |

| ice breaker | ледоломац (м) | ledolomac |
| submarine | подморница (ж) | podmornica |

boat (flat-bottomed ~)	чамац (м)	čamac
dinghy	чамчић (м)	čamčić
lifeboat	чамац (м) за спасавање	čamac za spasavanje
motorboat	моторни чамац (м)	motorni čamac

captain	капетан (м)	kapetan
seaman	морнар (м)	mornar
sailor	поморац (м)	pomorac
crew	посада (ж)	posada

boatswain	боцман (м)	bocman
ship's boy	бродски момак (м)	brodski momak
cook	кувар (м)	kuvar
ship's doctor	бродски лекар (м)	brodski lekar
deck	палуба (ж)	paluba

mast	јарбол (м)	jarbol
sail	једро (с)	jedro
hold	потпалубље (с)	potpalublje
bow (prow)	прамац (м)	pramac
stern	крма (ж)	krma
oar	весло (с)	veslo
screw propeller	бродски пропелер (м)	brodski propeler

cabin	кабина (ж)	kabina
wardroom	официрска менза (ж)	oficirska menza
engine room	стројарница (ж)	strojarnica
bridge	капетански мост (м)	kapetanski most
radio room	радио кабина (ж)	radio kabina
wave (radio)	талас (м)	talas
logbook	бродски дневник (м)	brodski dnevnik

spyglass	дурбин (м)	durbin
bell	звоно (с)	zvono
flag	застава (ж)	zastava

| hawser (mooring ~) | конопац (м) | konopac |
| knot (bowline, etc.) | чвор (м) | čvor |

| deckrails | ограда (ж) | ograda |
| gangway | степениште (с мн) | stepenište |

anchor	сидро (с)	sidro
to weigh anchor	дићи сидро	dići sidro
to drop anchor	спустити сидро	spustiti sidro
anchor chain	ланац (м) за сидро	lanac za sidro

port (harbor)	лука (ж)	luka
quay, wharf	пристаниште (с)	pristanište
to berth (moor)	усидрити се	usidriti se
to cast off	отиснути се	otisnuti se

trip, voyage	путовање (с)	putovanje
cruise (sea trip)	крстарење (с)	krstarenje
course (route)	правац (м)	pravac
route (itinerary)	маршрута (ж)	maršruta

fairway (safe water channel)	пловни пут (м)	plovni put
shallows	плићаци (м мн)	plićaci
to run aground	насукати се	nasukati se

storm	олуја (ж)	oluja
signal	сигнал (м)	signal
to sink (vi)	тонути	tonuti
Man overboard!	Човек у мору!	Čovek u moru!
SOS (distress signal)	СОС	SOS
ring buoy	појас (м) за спасавање	pojas za spasavanje

CITY

T&P Books Publishing

bus	аутобус (м)	autobus
streetcar	трамвај (м)	tramvaj
trolley bus	тролејбус (м)	trolejbus
route (of bus, etc.)	маршрута (ж)	maršruta
number (e.g., bus ~)	број (м)	broj

to go by ...	ићи ..., возити се ...	ići ..., voziti se ...
to get on (~ the bus)	ући у ...	ući u ...
to get off ...	сићи, изаћи из ...	sići, izaći iz ...

stop (e.g., bus ~)	станица (ж)	stanica
next stop	следећа станица (ж)	sledeća stanica
terminus	последња станица (ж)	poslednja stanica
schedule	ред (м) вожње	red vožnje
to wait (vt)	чекати	čekati

| ticket | карта (ж) | karta |
| fare | цена (ж) вожње | cena vožnje |

cashier (ticket seller)	благајник (м)	blagajnik
ticket inspection	контрола (ж) карата	kontrola karata
ticket inspector	контролор (м)	kontrolor

to be late (for ...)	каснити	kasniti
to miss (~ the train, etc.)	пропустити	propustiti
to be in a hurry	журити	žuriti

taxi, cab	такси (м)	taksi
taxi driver	таксиста (м)	taksista
by taxi	таксијем	taksijem
taxi stand	такси-станица (ж)	taksi-stanica
to call a taxi	позвати такси	pozvati taksi
to take a taxi	узети такси	uzeti taksi

traffic	саобраћај (м)	saobraćaj
traffic jam	застој (м) саобраћаја	zastoj saobraćaja
rush hour	шпиц (м)	špic
to park (vi)	паркирати се	parkirati se
to park (vt)	паркирати	parkirati
parking lot	паркинг (м)	parking

subway	метро (м)	metro
station	станица (ж)	stanica
to take the subway	ићи метроом	ići metroom

| train | воз (м) | voz |
| train station | железничка станица (ж) | železnička stanica |

28. City. Life in the city

city, town	град (м)	grad
capital city	главни град (м)	glavni grad
village	село (с)	selo

city map	план (м) града	plan grada
downtown	центар (м) града	centar grada
suburb	предграђе (с)	predgrađe
suburban (adj)	предградски	predgradski

outskirts	предграђе (с)	predgrađe
environs (suburbs)	околине (ж мн)	okoline
city block	кварт (м)	kvart
residential block (area)	стамбени кварт (м)	stambeni kvart

traffic	саобраћај (м)	saobraćaj
traffic lights	семафор (м)	semafor
public transportation	градски превоз (м)	gradski prevoz
intersection	раскрсница (ж)	raskrsnica

crosswalk	пешачки прелаз (м)	pešački prelaz
pedestrian underpass	подземни пролаз (м)	podzemni prolaz
to cross (~ the street)	прелазити	prelaziti
pedestrian	пешак (м)	pešak
sidewalk	тротоар (м)	trotoar

bridge	мост (м)	most
embankment (river walk)	кеј (м)	kej
fountain	водоскок (м)	vodoskok

allée (garden walkway)	алеја (ж)	aleja
park	парк (м)	park
boulevard	булевар (м)	bulevar
square	трг (м)	trg
avenue (wide street)	авенија (ж)	avenija
street	улица (ж)	ulica
side street	сокак (м)	sokak
dead end	ћорсокак (м)	ćorsokak

house	кућа (ж)	kuća
building	зграда (ж)	zgrada
skyscraper	небодер (м)	neboder

facade	фасада (с)	fasada
roof	кров (м)	krov
window	прозор (м)	prozor

arch	лук (м)	luk
column	колона (ж)	kolona
corner	угао (м)	ugao

store window	излог (м)	izlog
signboard (store sign, etc.)	натпис (м)	natpis
poster	плакат (м)	plakat
advertising poster	рекламни плакат (м)	reklamni plakat
billboard	билборд (м)	bilbord

garbage, trash	ђубре (с)	đubre
trashcan (public ~)	канта (ж) за ђубре	kanta za đubre
to litter (vi)	бацати ђубре	bacati đubre
garbage dump	депонија (ж)	deponija

phone booth	телефонска говорница (ж)	telefonska govornica
lamppost	стуб (м)	stub
bench (park ~)	клупа (ж)	klupa

police officer	полицајац (м)	policajac
police	полиција (ж)	policija
beggar	просјак (м)	prosjak
homeless (n)	бескућник (м)	beskućnik

29. Urban institutions

store	продавница (ж)	prodavnica
drugstore, pharmacy	апотека (ж)	apoteka
eyeglass store	оптика (ж)	optika
shopping mall	тржни центар (м)	tržni centar
supermarket	супермаркет (м)	supermarket

bakery	пекара (ж)	pekara
baker	пекар (м)	pekar
pastry shop	посластичарница (ж)	poslastičarnica
grocery store	бакалница (ж)	bakalnica
butcher shop	касапница (ж)	kasapnica

| produce store | пиљарница (ж) | piljarnica |
| market | пијаца (ж) | pijaca |

coffee house	кафана (ж)	kafana
restaurant	ресторан (м)	restoran
pub, bar	пивница (ж)	pivnica
pizzeria	пицерија (ж)	picerija

hair salon	фризерски салон (м)	frizerski salon
post office	пошта (ж)	pošta
dry cleaners	хемијско чишћење (с)	hemijsko čišćenje

photo studio	фотографска радња (ж)	fotografska radnja
shoe store	продавница (ж) обуће	prodavnica obuće
bookstore	књижара (ж)	knjižara
sporting goods store	продавница (ж) спортске опреме	prodavnica sportske opreme
clothes repair shop	кројачка (ж) радња	krojačka radnja
formal wear rental	изнајмљивање (с) одела	iznajmljivanje odela
video rental store	видео клуб (м)	video klub
circus	циркус (м)	cirkus
zoo	зоолошки врт (м)	zoološki vrt
movie theater	биоскоп (м)	bioskop
museum	музеј (м)	muzej
library	библиотека (ж)	biblioteka
theater	позориште (с)	pozorište
opera (opera house)	опера (ж)	opera
nightclub	ноћни клуб (м)	noćni klub
casino	казино (м)	kazino
mosque	џамија (ж)	džamija
synagogue	синагога (ж)	sinagoga
cathedral	катедрала (ж)	katedrala
temple	храм (м)	hram
church	црква (ж)	crkva
college	институт (м)	institut
university	универзитет (м)	univerzitet
school	школа (ж)	škola
prefecture	управа (ж)	uprava
city hall	градска кућа (ж)	gradska kuća
hotel	хотел (м)	hotel
bank	банка (ж)	banka
embassy	амбасада (ж)	ambasada
travel agency	туристичка агенција (ж)	turistička agencija
information office	биро (м) за информације	biro za informacije
currency exchange	мењачица (ж)	menjačica
subway	метро (с)	metro
hospital	болница (ж)	bolnica
gas station	бензинска станица (ж)	benzinska stanica
parking lot	паркинг (м)	parking

30. Signs

signboard (store sign, etc.)	натпис (м)	natpis
notice (door sign, etc.)	натпис (м), обавештење (с)	natpis, obaveštenje

poster	плакат (м)	plakat
direction sign	путоказ (м)	putokaz
arrow (sign)	стрелица (ж)	strelica

caution	упозорење (с)	upozorenje
warning sign	знак (м) упозорења	znak upozorenja
to warn (vt)	упозорити	upozoriti

rest day (weekly ~)	нерадни дан (м)	neradni dan
timetable (schedule)	распоред (м)	raspored
opening hours	радно време (с)	radno vreme

WELCOME!	ДОБРО ДОШЛИ!	DOBRO DOŠLI!
ENTRANCE	УЛАЗ	ULAZ
EXIT	ИЗЛАЗ	IZLAZ

PUSH	ГУРНИ	GURNI
PULL	ВУЦИ	VUCI
OPEN	ОТВОРЕНО	OTVORENO
CLOSED	ЗАТВОРЕНО	ZATVORENO

| WOMEN | ЖЕНЕ | ŽENE |
| MEN | МУШКАРЦИ | MUŠKARCI |

DISCOUNTS	ПОПУСТИ	POPUSTI
SALE	РАСПРОДАЈА	RASPRODAJA
NEW!	НОВО!	NOVO!
FREE	БЕСПЛАТНО	BESPLATNO

ATTENTION!	ПАЖЊА!	PAŽNJA!
NO VACANCIES	НЕМА СЛОБОДНИХ СОБА	NEMA SLOBODNIH SOBA
RESERVED	РЕЗЕРВИСАНО	REZERVISANO

| ADMINISTRATION | КАНЦЕЛАРИЈЕ | KANCELARIJE |
| STAFF ONLY | САМО ЗА ОСОБЉЕ | SAMO ZA OSOBLJE |

BEWARE OF THE DOG!	ЧУВАЈ СЕ ПСА	ČUVAJ SE PSA
NO SMOKING	ЗАБРАЊЕНО ПУШЕЊЕ	ZABRANJENO PUŠENJE
DO NOT TOUCH!	НЕ ДИРАЈ!	NE DIRAJ!

DANGEROUS	ОПАСНО	OPASNO
DANGER	ОПАСНОСТ	OPASNOST
HIGH VOLTAGE	ВИСОКИ НАПОН	VISOKI NAPON

| NO SWIMMING! | ЗАБРАЊЕНО КУПАЊЕ | ZABRANJENO KUPANJE |
| OUT OF ORDER | НЕ РАДИ | NE RADI |

FLAMMABLE	ЗАПАЉИВО	ZAPALJIVO
FORBIDDEN	ЗАБРАЊЕНО	ZABRANJENO
NO TRESPASSING!	ПРОЛАЗ ЗАБРАЊЕН!	PROLAZ ZABRANJEN!
WET PAINT	СВЕЖЕ ОФАРБАНО	SVEŽE OFARBANO

31. Shopping

to buy (purchase)	куповати	kupovati
purchase	куповина (ж)	kupovina
to go shopping	ићи у куповину	ići u kupovinu
shopping	куповина (ж)	kupovina
to be open (ab. store)	бити отворен	biti otvoren
to be closed	бити затворен	biti zatvoren
footwear, shoes	обућа (ж)	obuća
clothes, clothing	одећа (ж)	odeća
cosmetics	козметика (ж)	kozmetika
food products	намирнице (ж мн)	namirnice
gift, present	поклон (м)	poklon
salesman	продавац (м)	prodavac
saleswoman	продавачица (ж)	prodavačica
check out, cash desk	благајна (ж)	blagajna
mirror	огледало (с)	ogledalo
counter (store ~)	тезга (ж)	tezga
fitting room	кабина (ж) за пробавање	kabina za probavanje
to try on	пробати	probati
to fit (ab. dress, etc.)	пристајати	pristajati
to like (I like …)	свиђати се	sviđati se
price	цена (ж)	cena
price tag	ценовник (м)	cenovnik
to cost (vt)	коштати	koštati
How much?	Колико?	Koliko?
discount	попуст (м)	popust
inexpensive (adj)	није скуп	nije skup
cheap (adj)	јефтин	jeftin
expensive (adj)	скуп	skup
It's expensive	То је скупо	To je skupo
rental (n)	изнајмљивање (с)	iznajmljivanje
to rent (~ a tuxedo)	изнајмити	iznajmiti
credit (trade credit)	кредит (м)	kredit
on credit (adv)	на кредит	na kredit

CLOTHING &
ACCESSORIES

T&P Books Publishing

32. Outerwear. Coats

clothes	одећа (ж)	odeća
outerwear	горња одећа (ж)	gornja odeća
winter clothing	зимска одећа (ж)	zimska odeća

coat (overcoat)	капут (м)	kaput
fur coat	бунда (ж)	bunda
fur jacket	кратка бунда (ж)	kratka bunda
down coat	перјана јакна (ж)	perjana jakna

jacket (e.g., leather ~)	јакна (ж)	jakna
raincoat (trenchcoat, etc.)	кишни мантил (м)	kišni mantil
waterproof (adj)	водоотпоран	vodootporan

33. Men's & women's clothing

shirt (button shirt)	кошуља (ж)	košulja
pants	панталоне (ж мн)	pantalone
jeans	фармерке (ж мн)	farmerke
suit jacket	сако (м)	sako
suit	одело (с)	odelo

dress (frock)	хаљина (ж)	haljina
skirt	сукња (ж)	suknja
blouse	блуза (ж)	bluza
knitted jacket (cardigan, etc.)	џемпер (м)	džemper
jacket (of woman's suit)	жакет (м)	žaket

T-shirt	мајица (ж)	majica
shorts (short trousers)	шортс (м)	šorts
tracksuit	спортски костим (м)	sportski kostim
bathrobe	баде мантил (м)	bade mantil
pajamas	пиџама (ж)	pidžama

| sweater | џемпер (м) | džemper |
| pullover | пуловер (м) | pulover |

vest	прслук (м)	prsluk
tailcoat	фрак (м)	frak
tuxedo	смокинг (м)	smoking
uniform	униформа (ж)	uniforma
workwear	радно одело (с)	radno odelo

| overalls | комбинезон (м) | kombinezon |
| coat (e.g., doctor's smock) | мантил (м) | mantil |

34. Clothing. Underwear

underwear	доње рубље (с)	donje rublje
boxers, briefs	боксерице (ж мн)	bokserice
panties	гаћице (ж мн)	gaćice
undershirt (A-shirt)	мајица (ж)	majica
socks	чарапе (ж мн)	čarape

nightgown	спаваћица (ж)	spavaćica
bra	грудњак (м)	grudnjak
knee highs (knee-high socks)	доколенице (ж мн)	dokolenice
pantyhose	грилонке (ж мн)	grilonke
stockings (thigh highs)	хулахопке (ж мн)	hulahopke
bathing suit	купаћи костим (м)	kupaći kostim

35. Headwear

hat	капа (ж)	kapa
fedora	шешир (м)	šešir
baseball cap	качкет (м)	kačket
flatcap	енглеска капа (ж)	engleska kapa

beret	беретка (ж)	beretka
hood	капуљача (ж)	kapuljača
panama hat	панама-шешир (м)	panama-šešir
knit cap (knitted hat)	плетена капа (ж)	pletena kapa

| headscarf | марама (ж) | marama |
| women's hat | женски шешир (м) | ženski šešir |

hard hat	кацига (ж)	kaciga
garrison cap	војничка капа, титовка (ж)	vojnička kapa, titovka
helmet	шлем (м)	šlem

| derby | полуцилиндар (м) | policilindar |
| top hat | цилиндар (м) | cilindar |

36. Footwear

| footwear | обућа (ж) | obuća |
| shoes (men's shoes) | ципеле (ж мн) | cipele |

shoes (women's shoes)	ципеле (ж мн)	cipele
boots (e.g., cowboy ~)	чизме (ж мн)	čizme
slippers	папуче (ж мн)	papuče
tennis shoes (e.g., Nike ~)	патике (ж мн)	patike
sneakers (e.g., Converse ~)	старке (ж мн)	starke
sandals	сандале (ж мн)	sandale
cobbler (shoe repairer)	обућар (м)	obućar
heel	потпетица (ж)	potpetica
pair (of shoes)	пар (м)	par
shoestring	пертла (ж)	pertla
to lace (vt)	шнирати	šnirati
shoehorn	кашика (ж) за ципеле	kašika za cipele
shoe polish	крема (ж) за обућу	krema za obuću

37. Personal accessories

gloves	рукавице (ж мн)	rukavice
mittens	рукавице (ж мн)	rukavice
scarf (muffler)	шал (м)	šal
glasses (eyeglasses)	наочари (м мн)	naočari
frame (eyeglass ~)	оквир (м)	okvir
umbrella	кишобран (м)	kišobran
walking stick	штап (м)	štap
hairbrush	четка (ж) за косу	četka za kosu
fan	лепеза (ж)	lepeza
tie (necktie)	краватa (ж)	kravata
bow tie	лептир-машна (ж)	leptir-mašna
suspenders	трегери (мн)	tregeri
handkerchief	џепна марамица (ж)	džepna maramica
comb	чешаљ (м)	češalj
barrette	шнала (ж)	šnala
hairpin	укосница (ж)	ukosnica
buckle	копча (ж)	kopča
belt	пас (м)	pas
shoulder strap	каиш (м)	kaiš
bag (handbag)	торба (ж)	torba
purse	ташна (ж)	tašna
backpack	ранац (м)	ranac

38. Clothing. Miscellaneous

fashion	мода (ж)	moda
in vogue (adj)	модеран	moderan
fashion designer	модни креатор (м)	modni kreator

collar	оковратник (м)	okovratnik
pocket	џеп (м)	džep
pocket (as adj)	џепни	džepni
sleeve	рукав (м)	rukav
hanging loop	вешалица (ж)	vešalica
fly (on trousers)	шлиц (м)	šlic

zipper (fastener)	рајсфешлус (м)	rajsfešlus
fastener	копча (ж)	kopča
button	дугме (с)	dugme
buttonhole	рупица (ж)	rupica
to come off (ab. button)	откинути се	otkinuti se

to sew (vi, vt)	шити	šiti
to embroider (vi, vt)	вести	vesti
embroidery	вез (м)	vez
sewing needle	игла (ж)	igla
thread	конац (м)	konac
seam	шав (м)	šav

to get dirty (vi)	искаљати се	iskaljati se
stain (mark, spot)	мрља (ж)	mrlja
to crease, crumple (vi)	изгужвати се	izgužvati se
to tear, to rip (vt)	поцепати	pocepati
clothes moth	мољац (м)	moljac

39. Personal care. Cosmetics

toothpaste	паста (ж) за зубе	pasta za zube
toothbrush	четкица (ж) за зубе	četkica za zube
to brush one's teeth	прати зубе	prati zube

razor	бријач (м)	brijač
shaving cream	крема (ж) за бријање	krema za brijanje
to shave (vi)	бријати се	brijati se

soap	сапун (м)	sapun
shampoo	шампон (м)	šampon

scissors	маказе (мн)	makaze
nail file	турпијица (ж) за нокте	turpijica za nokte
nail clippers	грицкалица (ж) за нокте	grickalica za nokte
tweezers	пинцета (ж)	pinceta

cosmetics	козметика (ж)	kozmetika
face mask	маска (ж) за лице	maska za lice
manicure	маникир (м)	manikir
to have a manicure	маникирати	manikirati
pedicure	педикир (м)	pedikir
make-up bag	несесер (м)	neseser
face powder	пудер (м)	puder
powder compact	пудријера (ж)	pudrijera
blusher	руменило (с)	rumenilo
perfume (bottled)	парфем (м)	parfem
toilet water (lotion)	тоалетна вода (ж)	toaletna voda
lotion	лосион (м)	losion
cologne	колоњска вода (ж)	kolonjska voda
eyeshadow	сенка (ж) за очи	senka za oči
eyeliner	оловка (ж) за очи	olovka za oči
mascara	маскара (ж)	maskara
lipstick	кармин (м)	karmin
nail polish, enamel	лак (м) за нокте	lak za nokte
hair spray	лак (м) за косу	lak za kosu
deodorant	дезодоранс (м)	dezodorans
cream	крема (ж)	krema
face cream	крема (ж) за лице	krema za lice
hand cream	крема (ж) за руке	krema za ruke
anti-wrinkle cream	крема (ж) против бора	krema protiv bora
day cream	дневна крема (ж)	dnevna krema
night cream	ноћна крема (ж)	noćna krema
day (as adj)	дневни	dnevni
night (as adj)	ноћни	noćni
tampon	тампон (м)	tampon
toilet paper (toilet roll)	тоалет папир (м)	toalet papir
hair dryer	фен (м)	fen

40. Watches. Clocks

watch (wristwatch)	сат (м)	sat
dial	бројчаник (м)	brojčanik
hand (of clock, watch)	казаљка (ж)	kazaljka
metal watch band	наруквица (ж)	narukvica
watch strap	каиш (м) за сат	kaiš za sat
battery	батерија (ж)	baterija
to be dead (battery)	испразнити се	isprazniti se
to change a battery	променити батерију	promeniti bateriju
to run fast	журити	žuriti

to run slow	каснити	kasniti
wall clock	зидни сат (м)	zidni sat
hourglass	пешчани сат (м)	peščani sat
sundial	сунчани часовник (м)	sunčani časovnik
alarm clock	будилник (м)	budilnik
watchmaker	часовничар (м)	časovničar
to repair (vt)	поправљати	popravljati

EVERYDAY EXPERIENCE

T&P Books Publishing

money	новац (м)	novac
currency exchange	размена (ж) валута	razmena valuta
exchange rate	курс (м)	kurs
ATM	банкомат (м)	bankomat
coin	новчић (м), кованица (ж)	novčić, kovanica
dollar	долар (м)	dolar
euro	евро (м)	evro
lira	лира (ж)	lira
Deutschmark	немачка марка (ж)	nemačka marka
franc	франак (м)	franak
pound sterling	фунта (ж)	funta
yen	јен (м)	jen
debt	дуг (м)	dug
debtor	дужник (м)	dužnik
to lend (money)	дати у зајам	dati u zajam
to borrow (vi, vt)	узети у зајам	uzeti u zajam
bank	банка (ж)	banka
account	рачун (м)	račun
to deposit (vt)	ставити	staviti
to deposit into the account	ставити на рачун	staviti na račun
to withdraw (vt)	подићи са рачуна	podići sa računa
credit card	кредитна карта (ж)	kreditna karta
cash	готов новац (м)	gotov novac
check	чек (м)	ček
to write a check	написати чек	napisati ček
checkbook	чековна књижица (ж)	čekovna knjižica
wallet	новчаник (м)	novčanik
change purse	новчаничић (м)	novčaničić
safe	сеф (м)	sef
heir	наследник (м)	naslednik
inheritance	наследство (с)	nasledstvo
fortune (wealth)	имовина (ж)	imovina
lease	закуп (м)	zakup
rent (money)	станарина (ж)	stanarina
to rent (sth from sb)	изнајмити	iznajmiti
price	цена (ж)	cena

| cost | вредност (ж) | vrednost |
| sum | износ (м) | iznos |

to spend (vt)	трошити	trošiti
expenses	трошкови (м мн)	troškovi
to economize (vi, vt)	штедети	štedeti
economical	штедљив	štedljiv

to pay (vi, vt)	платити	platiti
payment	плаћање (с)	plaćanje
change (give the ~)	кусур (м)	kusur

tax	порез (м)	porez
fine	новчана казна (ж)	novčana kazna
to fine (vt)	казнити	kazniti

42. Post. Postal service

post office	пошта (ж)	pošta
mail (letters, etc.)	пошта (ж)	pošta
mailman	поштар (м)	poštar
opening hours	радно време (с)	radno vreme

letter	писмо (с)	pismo
registered letter	препоручено писмо (м)	preporučeno pismo
postcard	разгледница (ж)	razglednica
telegram	телеграм (м)	telegram
package (parcel)	пошиљка (ж)	pošiljka
money transfer	трансфер (м) новца	transfer novca

to receive (vt)	примити	primiti
to send (vt)	послати	poslati
sending	слање (с)	slanje
address	адреса (ж)	adresa
ZIP code	поштански број (м)	poštanski broj
sender	пошиљалац (м)	pošiljalac
receiver	прималац (м)	primalac

| name (first name) | име (с) | ime |
| surname (last name) | презиме (с) | prezime |

postage rate	поштарина (ж)	poštarina
standard (adj)	обичан	običan
economical (adj)	економичан	ekonomičan

weight	тежина (ж)	težina
to weigh (~ letters)	вагати	vagati
envelope	коверат (м)	koverat
postage stamp	поштанска марка (ж)	poštanska marka
to stamp an envelope	лепити марку	lepiti marku

43. Banking

bank	банка (ж)	banka
branch (of bank, etc.)	експозитура (ж)	ekspozitura
bank clerk, consultant	банкарски службеник (м)	bankarski službenik
manager (director)	менаџер (м)	menadžer
bank account	рачун (м)	račun
account number	број (м) рачуна	broj računa
checking account	текући рачун (м)	tekući račun
savings account	штедни рачун (м)	štedni račun
to open an account	отворити рачун	otvoriti račun
to close the account	затворити рачун	zatvoriti račun
to deposit into the account	ставити на рачун	staviti na račun
to withdraw (vt)	подићи са рачуна	podići sa računa
deposit	депозит (м)	depozit
to make a deposit	ставити новац на рачун	staviti novac na račun
wire transfer	трансфер (м) новца	transfer novca
to wire, to transfer	послати новац	poslati novac
sum	износ (м)	iznos
How much?	Колико?	Koliko?
signature	потпис (м)	potpis
to sign (vt)	потписати	potpisati
credit card	кредитна картица (ж)	kreditna kartica
code (PIN code)	код (м)	kod
credit card number	број (м) кредитне картице	broj kreditne kartice
ATM	банкомат (м)	bankomat
check	чек (м)	ček
to write a check	написати чек	napisati ček
checkbook	чековна књижица (ж)	čekovna knjižica
loan (bank ~)	кредит (м)	kredit
to apply for a loan	тражити кредит	tražiti kredit
to get a loan	подићи кредит	podići kredit
to give a loan	давати кредит	davati kredit
guarantee	гаранција (ж)	garancija

44. Telephone. Phone conversation

telephone	телефон (м)	telefon
cell phone	мобилни телефон (м)	mobilni telefon

answering machine	секретарица (ж)	sekretarica
to call (by phone)	звати	zvati
phone call	телефонски позив (м)	telefonski poziv

to dial a number	бирати број	birati broj
Hello!	Хало!	Halo!
to ask (vt)	упитати	upitati
to answer (vi, vt)	јавити се	javiti se

to hear (vt)	чути	čuti
well (adv)	добро	dobro
not well (adv)	лоше	loše
noises (interference)	звуци (м мн)	zvuci

receiver	слушалица (ж)	slušalica
to pick up (~ the phone)	подићи слушалицу	podići slušalicu
to hang up (~ the phone)	спустити слушалицу	spustiti slušalicu

busy (engaged)	заузето	zauzeto
to ring (ab. phone)	звонити	zvoniti
telephone book	телефонски именик (м)	telefonski imenik

local (adj)	локалан	lokalan
local call	локални позив (м)	lokalni poziv
long distance (~ call)	међуградски	međugradski
long-distance call	међуградски позив (м)	međugradski poziv
international (adj)	међународни	međunarodni
international call	међународни позив (м)	međunarodni poziv

45. Cell phone

cell phone	мобилни телефон (м)	mobilni telefon
display	дисплеј (м)	displej
button	дугме (с)	dugme
SIM card	СИМ картица (ж)	SIM kartica

battery	батерија (ж)	baterija
to be dead (battery)	испразнити се	isprazniti se
charger	пуњач (м)	punjač

menu	мени (м)	meni
settings	подешавања (с мн)	podešavanja
tune (melody)	мелодија (ж)	melodija
to select (vt)	изабрати	izabrati

calculator	дигитрон, калкулатор (м)	digitron, kalkulator
voice mail	говорна пошта (ж)	govorna pošta
alarm clock	аларм (м)	alarm
contacts	контакти (м мн)	kontakti

| SMS (text message) | СМС порука (ж) | SMS poruka |
| subscriber | претплатник (м) | pretplatnik |

46. Stationery

| ballpoint pen | хемијска оловка (ж) | hemijska olovka |
| fountain pen | наливперо (с) | nalivpero |

pencil	оловка (ж)	olovka
highlighter	маркер (м)	marker
felt-tip pen	фломастер (м)	flomaster

| notepad | нотес (м) | notes |
| agenda (diary) | роковник (м) | rokovnik |

ruler	лењир (м)	lenjir
calculator	дигитрон,	digitron,
	калкулатор (м)	kalkulator

eraser	гумица (ж)	gumica
thumbtack	ексерчић (ж)	ekserčić
paper clip	спајалица (ж)	spajalica

glue	лепак (м)	lepak
stapler	хефталица (ж)	heftalica
hole punch	бушилица (ж) за папир	bušilica za papir
pencil sharpener	резач (м)	rezač

47. Foreign languages

language	језик (м)	jezik
foreign (adj)	страни	strani
foreign language	страни језик (м)	strani jezik
to study (vt)	студирати	studirati
to learn (language, etc.)	учити	učiti

to read (vi, vt)	читати	čitati
to speak (vi, vt)	говорити	govoriti
to understand (vt)	разумети	razumeti
to write (vt)	писати	pisati

fast (adv)	брзо	brzo
slowly (adv)	споро	sporo
fluently (adv)	течно	tečno

rules	правила (с мн)	pravila
grammar	граматика (ж)	gramatika
vocabulary	лексикон (м)	leksikon
phonetics	фонетика (ж)	fonetika

textbook	уџбеник (м)	udžbenik
dictionary	речник (м)	rečnik
teach-yourself book	приручник (м) за самоуке	priručnik za samouke
phrasebook	приручник (м) за конверзацију	priručnik za konverzaciju

cassette, tape	касета (ж)	kaseta
videotape	видео касета (ж)	video kaseta
CD, compact disc	ЦД, диск (м)	CD, disk
DVD	ДВД (м)	DVD

alphabet	азбука, абецеда (ж)	azbuka, abeceda
to spell (vt)	спеловати	spelovati
pronunciation	изговор (м)	izgovor

accent	нагласак (м)	naglasak
with an accent	са нагласком	sa naglaskom
without an accent	без нагласка	bez naglaska

word	реч (ж)	reč
meaning	смисао (м)	smisao

course (e.g., a French ~)	течај (м)	tečaj
to sign up	уписати се	upisati se
teacher	професор (м)	profesor

translation (process)	превођење (с)	prevođenje
translation (text, etc.)	превод (м)	prevod
translator	преводилац (м)	prevodilac
interpreter	преводилац (м)	prevodilac

polyglot	полиглота (м)	poliglota
memory	памћење (с)	pamćenje

MEALS. RESTAURANT

T&P Books Publishing

48. Table setting

spoon	кашика (ж)	kašika
knife	нож (м)	nož
fork	виљушка (ж)	viljuška
cup (e.g., coffee ~)	шоља (ж)	šolja
plate (dinner ~)	тањир (м)	tanjir
saucer	тацна (ж)	tacna
napkin (on table)	салвета (ж)	salveta
toothpick	чачкалица (ж)	čačkalica

49. Restaurant

restaurant	ресторан (м)	restoran
coffee house	кафић (м)	kafić
pub, bar	бар (м)	bar
tearoom	чајџиница (ж)	čajdžinica
waiter	конобар (м)	konobar
waitress	конобарица (ж)	konobarica
bartender	бармен (м)	barmen
menu	јеловник (м)	jelovnik
wine list	винска карта (ж)	vinska karta
to book a table	резервисати сто	rezervisati sto
course, dish	јело (с)	jelo
to order (meal)	наручити	naručiti
to make an order	поручити	poručiti
aperitif	аперитив (м)	aperitiv
appetizer	предјело (с)	predjelo
dessert	десерт (м)	desert
check	рачун (м)	račun
to pay the check	исплатити рачун	isplatiti račun
to give change	вратити кусур	vratiti kusur
tip	бакшиш (м)	bakšiš

50. Meals

food	храна (ж)	hrana
to eat (vi, vt)	јести	jesti

breakfast	доручак (м)	doručak
to have breakfast	доручковати	doručkovati
lunch	ручак (м)	ručak
to have lunch	ручати	ručati
dinner	вечера (ж)	večera
to have dinner	вечерати	večerati

| appetite | апетит (м) | apetit |
| Enjoy your meal! | Пријатно! | Prijatno! |

to open (~ a bottle)	отварати	otvarati
to spill (liquid)	просути	prosuti
to spill out (vi)	просути се	prosuti se

to boil (vi)	кључати	ključati
to boil (vt)	проврити	provriti
boiled (~ water)	кључала	ključala
to chill, cool down (vt)	охладити	ohladiti
to chill (vi)	охладити се	ohladiti se

| taste, flavor | укус (м) | ukus |
| aftertaste | паукус (м) | paukus |

to slim down (lose weight)	мршавити	mršaviti
diet	дијета (ж)	dijeta
vitamin	витамин (м)	vitamin
calorie	калорија (ж)	kalorija
vegetarian (n)	вегетаријанац (м)	vegetarijanac
vegetarian (adj)	вегетаријански	vegetarijanski

fats (nutrient)	масти (ж мн)	masti
proteins	протеини, беланчевине (мн)	proteini, belančevine
carbohydrates	угљени хидрати (м мн)	ugljeni hidrati
slice (of lemon, ham)	парче (с)	parče
piece (of cake, pie)	комад (м)	komad
crumb (of bread, cake, etc.)	мрва (ж)	mrva

51. Cooked dishes

course, dish	јело (с)	jelo
cuisine	кухиња (ж)	kuhinja
recipe	рецепт (м)	recept
portion	порција (ж)	porcija

salad	салата (ж)	salata
soup	супа (ж)	supa
clear soup (broth)	буљон (м)	buljon
sandwich (bread)	сендвич (м)	sendvič

fried eggs	печена jaja (ж мн)	pečena jaja
hamburger (beefburger)	хамбургер (м)	hamburger
beefsteak	бифтек (м)	biftek

side dish	прилог (м)	prilog
spaghetti	шпагети (м мн)	špageti
mashed potatoes	пире (м) од кромпира	pire od krompira
pizza	пица (ж)	pica
porridge (oatmeal, etc.)	каша (ж)	kaša
omelet	омлет (м)	omlet

boiled (e.g., ~ beef)	куван	kuvan
smoked (adj)	димљен	dimljen
fried (adj)	пржен	pržen
dried (adj)	сушен	sušen
frozen (adj)	замрзнут	zamrznut
pickled (adj)	мариниран, укисељен	mariniran, ukiseljen

sweet (sugary)	сладак	sladak
salty (adj)	слан	slan
cold (adj)	хладан	hladan
hot (adj)	врућ	vruć
bitter (adj)	горак	gorak
tasty (adj)	укусан	ukusan

to cook in boiling water	барити	bariti
to cook (dinner)	кувати	kuvati
to fry (vt)	пржети	pržeti
to heat up (food)	подгревати	podgrevati

to salt (vt)	солити	soliti
to pepper (vt)	биберити	biberiti
to grate (vt)	рендати	rendati
peel (n)	кора (ж)	kora
to peel (vt)	љуштити	ljuštiti

52. Food

meat	месо (с)	meso
chicken	пилетина (ж)	piletina
Rock Cornish hen (poussin)	млада пилетина (ж)	mlada piletina
duck	патка (ж)	patka
goose	гуска (ж)	guska
game	дивљач (ж)	divljač
turkey	ћуран (м)	ćuran

pork	свињетина (ж)	svinjetina
veal	телетина (ж)	teletina
lamb	jaгњетина (ж)	jagnjetina

| beef | говедина (ж) | govedina |
| rabbit | зец (м) | zec |

sausage (bologna, pepperoni, etc.)	кобасица (ж)	kobasica
vienna sausage (frankfurter)	виршла (ж)	viršla
bacon	сланина (ж)	slanina
ham	шунка (ж)	šunka
gammon	димљена шунка (ж)	dimljena šunka

pâté	паштета (ж)	pašteta
liver	џигерица (ж)	džigerica
hamburger (ground beef)	млевено месо (с)	mleveno meso
tongue	језик (м)	jezik

egg	јаје (с)	jaje
eggs	јаја (с мн)	jaja
egg white	беланце (с)	belance
egg yolk	жуманце (с)	žumance

fish	риба (ж)	riba
seafood	плодови (м мн) мора	plodovi mora
crustaceans	ракови (м мн)	rakovi
caviar	кавијар (м)	kavijar

crab	морски рак (м)	morski rak
shrimp	морски рачић (м)	morski račić
oyster	острига (ж)	ostriga
spiny lobster	јастог (м)	jastog
octopus	октопод (м)	oktopod
squid	лигња (ж)	lignja

sturgeon	јесетрина (ж)	jesetrina
salmon	лосос (м)	losos
halibut	иверак (м)	iverak

cod	бакалар (м)	bakalar
mackerel	скуша (ж)	skuša
tuna	туњевина (ж)	tunjevina
eel	јегуља (ж)	jegulja

trout	пастрмка (ж)	pastrmka
sardine	сардина (ж)	sardina
pike	штука (ж)	štuka
herring	харинга (ж)	haringa

bread	хлеб (м)	hleb
cheese	сир (м)	sir
sugar	шећер (м)	šećer
salt	со (ж)	so
rice	пиринач (м)	pirinač

pasta (macaroni)	макароне (ж мн)	makarone
noodles	резанци (м мн)	rezanci
butter	маслац (м)	maslac
vegetable oil	зејтин (м)	zejtin
sunflower oil	сунцокретово уље (с)	suncokretovo ulje
margarine	маргарин (м)	margarin
olives	маслине (ж мн)	masline
olive oil	маслиново уље (с)	maslinovo ulje
milk	млеко (с)	mleko
condensed milk	кондензовано млеко (с)	kondenzovano mleko
yogurt	јогурт (м)	jogurt
sour cream	кисела павлака (ж)	kisela pavlaka
cream (of milk)	павлака (ж)	pavlaka
mayonnaise	мајонез (м)	majonez
buttercream	крем (м)	krem
cereal grains (wheat, etc.)	житарице (ж мн)	žitarice
flour	брашно (с)	brašno
canned food	конзервирана храна (ж)	konzervirana hrana
cornflakes	кукурузне пахуљице (ж мн)	kukuruzne pahuljice
honey	мед (м)	med
jam	џем (м)	džem
chewing gum	гума (ж) за жвакање	guma za žvakanje

53. Drinks

water	вода (ж)	voda
drinking water	вода (ж) за пиће	voda za piće
mineral water	кисела вода (ж)	kisela voda
still (adj)	негазирана	negazirana
carbonated (adj)	газирана	gazirana
sparkling (adj)	газирана	gazirana
ice	лед (м)	led
with ice	са ледом	sa ledom
non-alcoholic (adj)	безалкохолан	bezalkoholan
soft drink	безалкохолано пиће (с)	bezalkoholano piće
refreshing drink	освежавајуће пиће (с)	osvežavajuće piće
lemonade	лимунада (ж)	limunada
liquors	алкохолно пиће (с)	alkoholno piće
wine	вино (с)	vino
white wine	бело вино (с)	belo vino

red wine	црно вино (c)	crno vino
liqueur	ликер (м)	liker
champagne	шампањац (м)	šampanjac
vermouth	вермут (м)	vermut
whiskey	виски (м)	viski
vodka	водка (ж)	vodka
gin	џин (м)	džin
cognac	коњак (м)	konjak
rum	рум (м)	rum
coffee	кафа (ж)	kafa
black coffee	црна кафа (ж)	crna kafa
coffee with milk	кафа (ж) са млеком	kafa sa mlekom
cappuccino	капућино (м)	kapućino
instant coffee	инстант кафа (ж)	instant kafa
milk	млеко (c)	mleko
cocktail	коктел (м)	koktel
milkshake	милкшејк (м)	milkšejk
juice	сок (м)	sok
tomato juice	сок (м) од парадајза	sok od paradajza
orange juice	сок од наранџе (м)	sok od narandže
freshly squeezed juice	цеђени сок (м)	ceđeni sok
beer	пиво (c)	pivo
light beer	светло пиво (c)	svetlo pivo
dark beer	тамно пиво (c)	tamno pivo
tea	чај (м)	čaj
black tea	црни чај (м)	crni čaj
green tea	зелени чај (м)	zeleni čaj

54. Vegetables

vegetables	поврће (c)	povrće
greens	зелениш (м)	zeleniš
tomato	парадајз (м)	paradajz
cucumber	краставац (м)	krastavac
carrot	шаргарепа (ж)	šargarepa
potato	кромпир (м)	krompir
onion	црни лук (м)	crni luk
garlic	бели лук, чешњак (м)	beli luk, češnjak
cabbage	купус (м)	kupus
cauliflower	карфиол (м)	karfiol
Brussels sprouts	прокељ (м)	prokelj
broccoli	броколи (м)	brokoli

beetroot	цвекла (ж)	cvekla
eggplant	плави патлиџан (м)	plavi patlidžan
zucchini	тиквица (ж)	tikvica
pumpkin	тиква (ж)	tikva
turnip	репа (ж)	repa
parsley	першун (м)	peršun
dill	мирођија (ж)	mirođija
lettuce	зелена салата (ж)	zelena salata
celery	целер (м)	celer
asparagus	шпаргла (ж)	špargla
spinach	спанаћ (м)	spanać
pea	грашак (м)	grašak
beans	махунарке (ж мн)	mahunarke
corn (maize)	кукуруз (м)	kukuruz
kidney bean	пасуљ (м)	pasulj
bell pepper	паприка (ж)	paprika
radish	ротквица (ж)	rotkvica
artichoke	артичока (ж)	artičoka

55. Fruits. Nuts

fruit	воћка (ж)	voćka
apple	јабука (ж)	jabuka
pear	крушка (ж)	kruška
lemon	лимун (м)	limun
orange	наранџа (ж)	narandža
strawberry (garden ~)	јагода (ж)	jagoda
mandarin	мандарина (ж)	mandarina
plum	шљива (ж)	šljiva
peach	бресква (ж)	breskva
apricot	кајсија (ж)	kajsija
raspberry	малина (ж)	malina
pineapple	ананас (м)	ananas
banana	банана (ж)	banana
watermelon	лубеница (ж)	lubenica
grape	грожђе (с)	grožđe
sour cherry	вишња (ж)	višnja
sweet cherry	трешња (ж)	trešnja
melon	диња (ж)	dinja
grapefruit	грејпфрут (м)	grejpfrut
avocado	авокадо (м)	avokado
papaya	папаја (ж)	papaja
mango	манго (м)	mango
pomegranate	нар (м)	nar

redcurrant	црвена рибизла (ж)	crvena ribizla
blackcurrant	црна рибизла (ж)	crna ribizla
gooseberry	огрозд (м)	ogrozd
bilberry	боровница (ж)	borovnica
blackberry	купина (ж)	kupina

raisin	суво грожђе (с)	suvo grožđe
fig	смоква (ж)	smokva
date	урма (ж)	urma

peanut	кикирики (м)	kikiriki
almond	бадем (м)	badem
walnut	орах (м)	orah
hazelnut	лешник (м)	lešnik
coconut	кокосов орах (м)	kokosov orah
pistachios	пистаћи (мн)	pistaći

56. Bread. Candy

bakers' confectionery (pastry)	посластичарски производи (м мн)	poslastičarski proizvodi
bread	хлеб (м)	hleb
cookies	бисквити (м мн)	biskviti

chocolate (n)	чоколада (ж)	čokolada
chocolate (as adj)	чоколадан	čokoladan
candy (wrapped)	бомбона (ж)	bombona
cake (e.g., cupcake)	колач (м)	kolač
cake (e.g., birthday ~)	торта (ж)	torta

| pie (e.g., apple ~) | пита (ж) | pita |
| filling (for cake, pie) | фил (м) | fil |

jam (whole fruit jam)	слатко (с)	slatko
marmalade	мармелада (ж)	marmelada
waffles	облатне (мн)	oblatne
ice-cream	сладолед (м)	sladoled
pudding	пудинг (м)	puding

57. Spices

salt	со (ж)	so
salty (adj)	слан	slan
to salt (vt)	солити	soliti

| black pepper | црни бибер (м) | crni biber |
| red pepper (milled ~) | црвени бибер (млевени) | crveni biber (mleveni) |

mustard	**сенф** (м)	senf
horseradish	**рен, хрен** (м)	ren, hren
condiment	**додатак, зачин** (м)	dodatak, začin
spice	**зачин** (м)	začin
sauce	**сос** (м)	sos
vinegar	**сирће** (с)	sirće
anise	**анис** (м)	anis
basil	**босиљак** (м)	bosiljak
cloves	**каранфил** (м)	karanfil
ginger	**ђумбир** (м)	đumbir
coriander	**кориандер** (м)	koriander
cinnamon	**цимет** (м)	cimet
sesame	**сусам** (м)	susam
bay leaf	**ловор** (м)	lovor
paprika	**паприка** (м)	paprika
caraway	**ким** (м)	kim
saffron	**шафран** (м)	šafran

PERSONAL
INFORMATION. FAMILY

T&P Books Publishing

58. Personal information. Forms

name (first name)	**име** (с)	ime
surname (last name)	**презиме** (с)	prezime
date of birth	**датум** (м) **рођења**	datum rođenja
place of birth	**место** (с) **рођења**	mesto rođenja
nationality	**националност** (ж)	nacionalnost
place of residence	**место** (с) **боравка**	mesto boravka
country	**земља** (ж)	zemlja
profession (occupation)	**професија** (ж)	profesija
gender, sex	**пол** (м)	pol
height	**раст** (м)	rast
weight	**тежина** (ж)	težina

59. Family members. Relatives

mother	**мајка** (ж)	majka
father	**отац** (м)	otac
son	**син** (м)	sin
daughter	**кћи** (ж)	kći
younger daughter	**млађа кћи** (ж)	mlađa kći
younger son	**млађи син** (м)	mlađi sin
eldest daughter	**најстарија кћи** (ж)	najstarija kći
eldest son	**најстарији син** (м)	najstariji sin
brother	**брат** (м)	brat
elder brother	**старији брат** (м)	stariji brat
younger brother	**млађи брат** (м)	mlađi brat
sister	**сестра** (ж)	sestra
elder sister	**старија сестра** (ж)	starija sestra
younger sister	**млађа сестра** (ж)	mlađa sestra
cousin (masc.)	**рођак** (м)	rođak
cousin (fem.)	**рођака** (ж)	rođaka
mom, mommy	**мама** (ж)	mama
dad, daddy	**тата** (м)	tata
parents	**родитељи** (мн)	roditelji
child	**дете** (с)	dete
children	**деца** (с мн)	deca
grandmother	**бака** (ж)	baka
grandfather	**деда** (м)	deda

grandson	унук (м)	unuk
granddaughter	унука (ж)	unuka
grandchildren	унуци (мн)	unuci

uncle	ујак, стриц (м)	ujak, stric
aunt	ујна, стрина (ж)	ujna, strina
nephew	синовац (м)	sinovac
niece	синовица (ж)	sinovica

mother-in-law (wife's mother)	ташта (ж)	tašta
father-in-law (husband's father)	свекар (м)	svekar
son-in-law (daughter's husband)	зет (м)	zet

| stepmother | маћеха (ж) | maćeha |
| stepfather | очух (м) | očuh |

infant	одојче (с)	odojče
baby (infant)	беба (ж)	beba
little boy, kid	мало дете (с)	malo dete

wife	жена (ж)	žena
husband	муж (м)	muž
spouse (husband)	супруг (м)	suprug
spouse (wife)	супруга (ж)	supruga

married (masc.)	ожењен	oženjen
married (fem.)	удата	udata
single (unmarried)	неожењен	neoženjen
bachelor	нежења (м)	neženja
divorced (masc.)	разведен	razveden
widow	удовица (ж)	udovica
widower	удовац (м)	udovac

relative	рођак (м)	rođak
close relative	блиски рођак (м)	bliski rođak
distant relative	даљи рођак (м)	dalji rođak
relatives	рођаци (мн)	rođaci

orphan (boy or girl)	сироче (с)	siroče
guardian (of a minor)	старатељ (м)	staratelj
to adopt (a boy)	усвојити	usvojiti
to adopt (a girl)	усвојити	usvojiti

60. Friends. Coworkers

friend (masc.)	пријатељ (м)	prijatelj
friend (fem.)	пријатељица (ж)	prijateljica
friendship	пријатељство (с)	prijateljstvo

to be friends	дружити се	družiti se
buddy (masc.)	пријатељ (м)	prijatelj
buddy (fem.)	пријатељица (ж)	prijateljica
partner	партнер (м)	partner

chief (boss)	шеф (м)	šef
superior (n)	начелник (м)	načelnik
owner, proprietor	власник (м)	vlasnik
subordinate (n)	подређени (м)	podređeni
colleague	колега (м)	kolega

acquaintance (person)	познаник (м)	poznanik
fellow traveler	сапутник (м)	saputnik
classmate	школски друг (м)	školski drug

neighbor (masc.)	комшија (м)	komšija
neighbor (fem.)	комшиница (ж)	komšinica
neighbors	комшије (мн)	komšije

HUMAN BODY. MEDICINE

T&P Books Publishing

61. Head

head	глава (ж)	glava
face	лице (с)	lice
nose	нос (м)	nos
mouth	уста (с мн)	usta

eye	око (с)	oko
eyes	очи (с мн)	oči
pupil	зеница (ж)	zenica
eyebrow	обрва (ж)	obrva
eyelash	трепавица (ж)	trepavica
eyelid	капак (м)	kapak

tongue	језик (м)	jezik
tooth	зуб (м)	zub
lips	усне (ж мн)	usne
cheekbones	јагодице (ж мн)	jagodice
gum	десни (с мн)	desni
palate	непце (с)	nepce

nostrils	ноздрве (ж мн)	nozdrve
chin	брада (ж)	brada
jaw	вилица (ж)	vilica
cheek	образ (м)	obraz

forehead	чело (с)	čelo
temple	слепоочница (ж)	slepoočnica
ear	ухо (с)	uho
back of the head	потиљак (м)	potiljak
neck	врат (м)	vrat
throat	грло (с)	grlo

hair	коса (ж)	kosa
hairstyle	фризура (ж)	frizura
haircut	фризура (ж)	frizura
wig	перика (ж)	perika

mustache	бркови (м мн)	brkovi
beard	брада (ж)	brada
to have (a beard, etc.)	носити	nositi
braid	плетеница (ж)	pletenica
sideburns	зулуфи (м мн)	zulufi

| red-haired (adj) | риђ | riđ |
| gray (hair) | сед | sed |

bald (adj)	**ћелав**	ćelav
bald patch	**ћела** (ж)	ćela
ponytail	**коњски реп** (м)	konjski rep
bangs	**шишке** (мн)	šiške

62. Human body

hand	**шака** (ж)	šaka
arm	**рука** (ж)	ruka
finger	**прст** (м)	prst
toe	**ножни прст** (м)	nožni prst
thumb	**палац** (м)	palac
little finger	**мали прст** (м)	mali prst
nail	**нокат** (м)	nokat
fist	**песница** (ж)	pesnica
palm	**длан** (ж)	dlan
wrist	**запешће** (с)	zapešće
forearm	**подлактица** (ж)	podlaktica
elbow	**лакат** (м)	lakat
shoulder	**раме** (с)	rame
leg	**нога** (ж)	noga
foot	**стопало** (с)	stopalo
knee	**колено** (с)	koleno
calf (part of leg)	**лист** (м)	list
hip	**кук** (м)	kuk
heel	**пета** (ж)	peta
body	**тело** (с)	telo
stomach	**трбух** (м)	trbuh
chest	**прса** (мн)	prsa
breast	**груди** (ж мн)	grudi
flank	**бок** (м)	bok
back	**леђа** (мн)	leđa
lower back	**крста** (с мн)	krsta
waist	**струк** (м)	struk
navel (belly button)	**пупак** (м)	pupak
buttocks	**стражњица** (ж)	stražnjica
bottom	**задњица** (ж)	zadnjica
beauty mark	**младеж** (м)	mladež
birthmark (café au lait spot)	**белег, младеж** (м)	beleg, mladež
tattoo	**тетоважа** (ж)	tetovaža
scar	**ожиљак** (м)	ožiljak

63. Diseases

sickness	болест (ж)	bolest
to be sick	боловати	bolovati
health	здравље (с)	zdravlje

runny nose (coryza)	кијавица (ж)	kijavica
tonsillitis	ангина (ж)	angina
cold (illness)	прехлада (ж)	prehlada
to catch a cold	прехладити се	prehladiti se

bronchitis	бронхитис (м)	bronhitis
pneumonia	запаљење (с) плућа	zapaljenje pluća
flu, influenza	грип (м)	grip

nearsighted (adj)	кратковид	kratkovid
farsighted (adj)	далековид	dalekovid
strabismus (crossed eyes)	разрокост (ж)	razrokost
cross-eyed (adj)	разрок	razrok
cataract	катаракта (ж)	katarakta
glaucoma	глауком (м)	glaukom

stroke	мождани удар (м)	moždani udar
heart attack	инфаркт (м)	infarkt
myocardial infarction	инфаркт (м) миокарда	infarkt miokarda
paralysis	парализа (ж)	paraliza
to paralyze (vt)	парализовати	paralizovati

allergy	алергија (ж)	alergija
asthma	астма (ж)	astma
diabetes	дијабетес (м)	dijabetes

toothache	зубобоља (ж)	zubobolja
caries	каријес (м)	karijes

diarrhea	дијареја (ж), пролив (м)	dijareja, proliv
constipation	затвор (м)	zatvor
stomach upset	лоша пробава (ж)	loša probava
food poisoning	тровање (с) храном	trovanje hranom
to get food poisoning	отровати се	otrovati se

arthritis	артритис (м)	artritis
rickets	рахитис (м)	rahitis
rheumatism	реуматизам (м)	reumatizam
atherosclerosis	атеросклероза (ж)	ateroskleroza

gastritis	гастритис (м)	gastritis
appendicitis	апендицитис (м)	apendicitis
cholecystitis	холециститис (м)	holecistitis
ulcer	чир (м) на желуцу	čir na želucu
measles	мале богиње (ж мн)	male boginje

rubella (German measles)	рубеола (ж)	rubeola
jaundice	жутица (ж)	žutica
hepatitis	хепатитис (м)	hepatitis

schizophrenia	шизофренија (ж)	šizofrenija
rabies (hydrophobia)	беснило (с)	besnilo
neurosis	неуроза (ж)	neuroza
concussion	потрес (м) мозга	potres mozga

cancer	рак (м)	rak
sclerosis	склероза (ж)	skleroza
multiple sclerosis	мултипла склероза (ж)	multipla skleroza

alcoholism	алкохолизам (м)	alkoholizam
alcoholic (n)	алкохоличар (м)	alkoholičar
syphilis	сифилис (м)	sifilis
AIDS	СИДА (ж)	SIDA

tumor	тумор (м)	tumor
malignant (adj)	малигни	maligni
benign (adj)	бенигни	benigni

fever	грозница (ж)	groznica
malaria	маларија (ж)	malarija
gangrene	гангрена (ж)	gangrena
seasickness	морска болест (ж)	morska bolest
epilepsy	епилепсија (ж)	epilepsija

epidemic	епидемија (ж)	epidemija
typhus	тифус (м)	tifus
tuberculosis	туберкулоза (ж)	tuberkuloza
cholera	колера (ж)	kolera
plague (bubonic ~)	куга (ж)	kuga

64. Symptoms. Treatments. Part 1

symptom	симптом (м)	simptom
temperature	температура (ж)	temperatura
high temperature (fever)	висока температура (ж)	visoka temperatura
pulse	пулс (м)	puls

dizziness (vertigo)	вртоглавица (ж)	vrtoglavica
hot (adj)	врућ	vruć
shivering	језа (ж)	jeza
pale (e.g., ~ face)	блед	bled

cough	кашаљ (м)	kašalj
to cough (vi)	кашљати	kašljati
to sneeze (vi)	кијати	kijati
faint	несвестица (ж)	nesvestica

to faint (vi)	онесвестити се	onesvestiti se
bruise (hématome)	модрица (ж)	modrica
bump (lump)	чворуга (ж)	čvoruga
to bang (bump)	ударити се	udariti se
contusion (bruise)	озледа (ж)	ozleda
to get a bruise	озледити се	ozlediti se
to limp (vi)	храмати	hramati
dislocation	ишчашење (с)	iščašenje
to dislocate (vt)	ишчашити	iščašiti
fracture	прелом (м)	prelom
to have a fracture	задобити прелом	zadobiti prelom
cut (e.g., paper ~)	посекотина (ж)	posekotina
to cut oneself	посећи се	poseći se
bleeding	крварење (с)	krvarenje
burn (injury)	опекотина (ж)	opekotina
to get burned	опећи се	opeći se
to prick (vt)	убости	ubosti
to prick oneself	убости се	ubosti se
to injure (vt)	повредити	povrediti
injury	повреда (ж)	povreda
wound	рана (ж)	rana
trauma	траума (ж)	trauma
to be delirious	бунцати	buncati
to stutter (vi)	муцати	mucati
sunstroke	сунчаница (ж)	sunčanica

65. Symptoms. Treatments. Part 2

pain, ache	бол (м)	bol
splinter (in foot, etc.)	трн (м)	trn
sweat (perspiration)	зној (м)	znoj
to sweat (perspire)	знојити се	znojiti se
vomiting	повраћање (с)	povraćanje
convulsions	конвулзије (ж мн)	konvulzije
pregnant (adj)	трудна	trudna
to be born	родити се	roditi se
delivery, labor	порођај (м)	porođaj
to deliver (~ a baby)	рађати	rađati
abortion	абортус (м), побачај (м)	abortus, pobačaj
breathing, respiration	дисање (с)	disanje
in-breath (inhalation)	удисај (м)	udisaj
out-breath (exhalation)	издисај (м)	izdisaj

| to exhale (breathe out) | издахнути | izdahnuti |
| to inhale (vi) | удахнути | udahnuti |

disabled person	инвалид (м)	invalid
cripple	богаљ (м)	bogalj
drug addict	наркоман (м)	narkoman

deaf (adj)	глув	gluv
mute (adj)	нем	nem
deaf mute (adj)	глувонем	gluvonem

mad, insane (adj)	луд	lud
madman (demented person)	лудак (м)	ludak
madwoman	луда (ж)	luda
to go insane	полудети	poludeti

gene	ген (м)	gen
immunity	имунитет (м)	imunitet
hereditary (adj)	наследни	nasledni
congenital (adj)	урођен	urođen

virus	вирус (м)	virus
microbe	микроб (м)	mikrob
bacterium	бактерија (ж)	bakterija
infection	инфекција (ж)	infekcija

66. Symptoms. Treatments. Part 3

| hospital | болница (ж) | bolnica |
| patient | пацијент (м) | pacijent |

diagnosis	дијагноза (ж)	dijagnoza
cure	лечење (с)	lečenje
medical treatment	медицински третман (м)	medicinski tretman
to get treatment	лечити се	lečiti se
to treat (~ a patient)	лечити	lečiti
to nurse (look after)	неговати	negovati
care (nursing ~)	неговање (с)	negovanje

operation, surgery	операција (ж)	operacija
to bandage (head, limb)	превити	previti
bandaging	превијање (с)	previjanje

vaccination	вакцинација (ж)	vakcinacija
to vaccinate (vt)	вакцинисати се	vakcinisati se
injection, shot	ињекција (ж)	injekcija
to give an injection	дати ињекцију	dati injekciju
attack	напад (м)	napad
amputation	ампутација (ж)	amputacija

to amputate (vt)	**ампутирати**	amputirati
coma	**кома** (ж)	koma
to be in a coma	**бити у коми**	biti u komi
intensive care	**интензивна нега** (ж)	intenzivna nega
to recover (~ from flu)	**опоравити**	oporaviti
condition (patient's ~)	**стање** (с)	stanje
consciousness	**свест** (ж)	svest
memory (faculty)	**памћење** (с)	pamćenje
to pull out (tooth)	**вадити**	vaditi
filling	**пломба** (ж)	plomba
to fill (a tooth)	**пломбирати**	plombirati
hypnosis	**хипноза** (ж)	hipnoza
to hypnotize (vt)	**хипнотисати**	hipnotisati

67. Medicine. Drugs. Accessories

medicine, drug	**лек** (м)	lek
remedy	**средство** (с)	sredstvo
to prescribe (vt)	**преписати**	prepisati
prescription	**рецепт** (м)	recept
tablet, pill	**таблета** (ж)	tableta
ointment	**маст** (ж)	mast
ampule	**ампула** (ж)	ampula
mixture	**микстура** (ж)	mikstura
syrup	**сируп** (м)	sirup
pill	**пилула** (ж)	pilula
powder	**прашак** (м)	prašak
gauze bandage	**завој** (м)	zavoj
cotton wool	**вата** (ж)	vata
iodine	**јод** (м)	jod
Band-Aid	**фластер** (м)	flaster
eyedropper	**пипета** (ж)	pipeta
thermometer	**термометар** (м)	termometar
syringe	**шприц** (м)	špric
wheelchair	**инвалидска колица** (ж)	invalidska kolica
crutches	**штаке** (ж мн)	štake
painkiller	**аналгетик** (м)	analgetik
laxative	**лаксатив** (м)	laksativ
spirits (ethanol)	**алкохол** (м)	alkohol
medicinal herbs	**лековито биље** (с)	lekovito bilje
herbal (~ tea)	**биљни**	biljni

APARTMENT

T&P Books Publishing

68. Apartment

apartment	стан (м)	stan
room	соба (ж)	soba
bedroom	спаваћа соба (ж)	spavaća soba
dining room	трпезарија (ж)	trpezarija
living room	дневна соба (ж)	dnevna soba
study (home office)	кабинет (м)	kabinet
entry room	предсобље (с)	predsoblje
bathroom (room with a bath or shower)	купатило (с)	kupatilo
half bath	тоалет (м)	toalet
ceiling	плафон (м)	plafon
floor	под (м)	pod
corner	угао (м)	ugao

69. Furniture. Interior

furniture	намештај (м)	nameštaj
table	сто (м)	sto
chair	столица (ж)	stolica
bed	кревет (м)	krevet
couch, sofa	диван (м)	divan
armchair	фотеља (ж)	fotelja
bookcase	орман (м) за књиге	orman za knjige
shelf	полица (ж)	polica
wardrobe	орман (м)	orman
coat rack (wall-mounted ~)	вешалица (ж)	vešalica
coat stand	чивилук (м)	čiviluk
bureau, dresser	комода (ж)	komoda
coffee table	клуб-сто (м)	klub-sto
mirror	огледало (с)	ogledalo
carpet	тепих (м)	tepih
rug, small carpet	простирка (ж)	prostirka
fireplace	камин (м)	kamin
candle	свећа (ж)	sveća
candlestick	свећњак (м)	svećnjak

drapes	завесе (ж мн)	zavese
wallpaper	тапете (ж мн)	tapete
blinds (jalousie)	ролетна (ж)	roletna

table lamp	стона лампа (ж)	stona lampa
wall lamp (sconce)	зидна лампа (ж)	zidna lampa
floor lamp	подна лампа (ж)	podna lampa
chandelier	лустер (м)	luster

leg (of chair, table)	нога (ж)	noga
armrest	наслон (м) за руке	naslon za ruke
back (backrest)	наслон (м)	naslon
drawer	фиока (ж)	fioka

70. Bedding

bedclothes	постељина (ж)	posteljina
pillow	јастук (м)	jastuk
pillowcase	јастучница (ж)	jastučnica
duvet, comforter	јорган (м)	jorgan
sheet	чаршав (м)	čaršav
bedspread	покривач (м)	pokrivač

71. Kitchen

kitchen	кухиња (ж)	kuhinja
gas	плин (м)	plin
gas stove (range)	плински шпорет (м)	plinski šporet
electric stove	електрички шпорет (м)	električki šporet
oven	рерна (ж)	rerna
microwave oven	микроталасна рерна (ж)	mikrotalasna rerna

refrigerator	фрижидер (м)	frižider
freezer	замрзивач (м)	zamrzivač
dishwasher	машина (ж)	mašina
	за прање судова	za pranje sudova

meat grinder	машина (ж)	mašina
	за млевење меса	za mlevenje mesa
juicer	соковник (м)	sokovnik
toaster	тостер (м)	toster
mixer	миксер (м)	mikser

coffee machine	аппарат (м) за кафу	apparat za kafu
coffee pot	лонче (с) за кафу	lonče za kafu
coffee grinder	апарат (м)	aparat
	за млевење кафе	za mlevenje kafe
kettle	кувало, чајник (м)	kuvalo, čajnik

teapot	чајник (м)	čajnik
lid	поклопац (м)	poklopac
tea strainer	цедиљка (ж)	cediljka

spoon	кашика (ж)	kašika
teaspoon	кашичица (ж)	kašičica
soup spoon	супена кашика (ж)	supena kašika
fork	виљушка (ж)	viljuška
knife	нож (м)	nož

tableware (dishes)	посуђе (с)	posuđe
plate (dinner ~)	тањир (м)	tanjir
saucer	тацна (ж)	tacna

shot glass	чашица (ж)	čašica
glass (tumbler)	чаша (ж)	čaša
cup	шоља (ж)	šolja

sugar bowl	шећерница (ж)	šećernica
salt shaker	сланик (м)	slanik
pepper shaker	биберница (ж)	bibernica
butter dish	посуда (ж) за маслац	posuda za maslac

stock pot (soup pot)	шерпа (ж)	šerpa
frying pan (skillet)	тигањ (м)	tiganj
ladle	кутлача (ж)	kutlača
colander	цедиљка (ж)	cediljka
tray (serving ~)	послужавник (м)	poslužavnik

bottle	боца (ж), флаша (ж)	boca, flaša
jar (glass)	тегла (ж)	tegla
can	лименка, конзерва (ж)	limenka, konzerva

bottle opener	отварач (м)	otvarač
can opener	отварач (м)	otvarač
corkscrew	вадичеп (м)	vadičep
filter	филтар (м)	filtar
to filter (vt)	филтровати	filtrovati

| trash, garbage (food waste, etc.) | отпаци (м мн), ђубре (с) | otpaci, đubre |
| trash can (kitchen ~) | канта (ж) за ђубре | kanta za đubre |

72. Bathroom

bathroom	купатило (с)	kupatilo
water	вода (ж)	voda
faucet	славина (ж)	slavina
hot water	топла вода (ж)	topla voda
cold water	хладна вода (ж)	hladna voda

toothpaste	паста (ж) за зубе	pasta za zube
to brush one's teeth	прати зубе	prati zube
toothbrush	четкица (ж) за зубе	četkica za zube
to shave (vi)	бријати се	brijati se
shaving foam	пена (ж) за бријање	pena za brijanje
razor	бријач (м)	brijač
to wash (one's hands, etc.)	прати	prati
to take a bath	купати се	kupati se
shower	туш (м)	tuš
to take a shower	туширати се	tuširati se
bathtub	када (ж)	kada
toilet (toilet bowl)	WC шоља (ж)	WC šolja
sink (washbasin)	лавабо (м)	lavabo
soap	сапун (м)	sapun
soap dish	кутија (ж) за сапун	kutija za sapun
sponge	сунђер (м)	sunđer
shampoo	шампон (м)	šampon
towel	пешкир (м)	peškir
bathrobe	баде мантил (м)	bade mantil
laundry (process)	прање (с) веша	pranje veša
washing machine	веш-машина (ж)	veš-mašina
to do the laundry	прати веш	prati veš
laundry detergent	прашак (м) за веш	prašak za veš

73. Household appliances

TV set	телевизор (м)	televizor
tape recorder	касетофон (м)	kasetofon
VCR (video recorder)	видео рекордер (м)	video rekorder
radio	радио (м)	radio
player (CD, MP3, etc.)	плејер (м)	plejer
video projector	видео пројектор (м)	video projektor
home movie theater	кућни биоскоп (м)	kućni bioskop
DVD player	ДВД плејер (м)	DVD plejer
amplifier	појачало (м)	pojačalo
video game console	конзола (ж)	konzola
	за видео игрице	za video igrice
video camera	видеокамера (ж)	videokamera
camera (photo)	фотоапарат (м)	fotoaparat
digital camera	дигитални	digitalni
	фотоапарат (м)	fotoaparat
vacuum cleaner	усисивач (м)	usisivač

iron (e.g., steam ~)	пегла (ж)	pegla
ironing board	даска (ж) за пеглање	daska za peglanje
telephone	телефон (м)	telefon
cell phone	мобилни телефон (м)	mobilni telefon
typewriter	писаћа машина (ж)	pisaća mašina
sewing machine	шиваћа машина (ж)	šivaća mašina
microphone	микрофон (м)	mikrofon
headphones	слушалице (ж мн)	slušalice
remote control (TV)	даљински управљач (м)	daljinski upravljač
CD, compact disc	ЦД, диск (м)	CD, disk
cassette, tape	касета (ж)	kaseta
vinyl record	плоча (ж)	ploča

THE EARTH. WEATHER

T&P Books Publishing

space	свемир (м)	svemir
space (as adj)	космички	kosmički
outer space	свемирски простор (м)	svemirski prostor
world	свет (м)	svet
universe	универзум (м)	univerzum
galaxy	галаксија (ж)	galaksija

star	звезда (ж)	zvezda
constellation	сажвежђе (с)	sažvežđe
planet	планета (ж)	planeta
satellite	сателит (м)	satelit

meteorite	метеорит (м)	meteorit
comet	комета (ж)	kometa
asteroid	астероид (м)	asteroid

orbit	орбита (ж)	orbita
to revolve (~ around the Earth)	окретати се	okretati se
atmosphere	атмосфера (ж)	atmosfera

the Sun	сунце (с)	sunce
solar system	Сунчев систем (м)	Sunčev sistem
solar eclipse	помрачење (с) сунца	pomračenje sunca

the Earth	Земља (ж)	Zemlja
the Moon	Месец (м)	Mesec

Mars	Марс (м)	Mars
Venus	Венера (ж)	Venera
Jupiter	Јупитер (м)	Jupiter
Saturn	Сатурн (м)	Saturn

Mercury	Меркур (м)	Merkur
Uranus	Уран (м)	Uran
Neptune	Нептун (м)	Neptun
Pluto	Плутон (м)	Pluton

Milky Way	Млечни пут (м)	Mlečni put
Great Bear (Ursa Major)	Велики медвед (м)	Veliki medved
North Star	Северњача (ж)	Severnjača

Martian	марсовац (м)	marsovac
extraterrestrial (n)	ванземаљац (м)	vanzemaljac

| alien | свемирац (м) | svemirac |
| flying saucer | летећи тањир (м) | leteći tanjir |

spaceship	свемирски брод (м)	svemirski brod
space station	орбитна станица (ж)	orbitna stanica
blast-off	лансирање (с)	lansiranje

engine	мотор (м)	motor
nozzle	млазница (ж)	mlaznica
fuel	гориво (с)	gorivo

cockpit, flight deck	кабина (ж)	kabina
antenna	антена (ж)	antena
porthole	бродски прозор (м)	brodski prozor
solar panel	соларни панел (м)	solarni panel
spacesuit	свемирско одело (с)	svemirsko odelo

| weightlessness | бестежинско стање (с) | bestežinsko stanje |
| oxygen | кисеоник (м) | kiseonik |

| docking (in space) | спајање, пристајање (с) | spajanje, pristajanje |
| to dock (vi, vt) | спајати | spajati |

observatory	опсерваторијум (м)	opservatorijum
telescope	телескоп (м)	teleskop
to observe (vt)	посматрати	posmatrati
to explore (vt)	истраживати	istraživati

75. The Earth

the Earth	Земља (ж)	Zemlja
the globe (the Earth)	земљина кугла (ж)	zemljina kugla
planet	планета (ж)	planeta

atmosphere	атмосфера (ж)	atmosfera
geography	географија (ж)	geografija
nature	природа (ж)	priroda

globe (table ~)	глобус (м)	globus
map	мапа (ж)	mapa
atlas	атлас (м)	atlas

Europe	Европа (ж)	Evropa
Asia	Азија (ж)	Azija
Africa	Африка (ж)	Afrika
Australia	Аустралија (ж)	Australija

America	Америка (ж)	Amerika
North America	Северна Америка (ж)	Severna Amerika
South America	Јужна Америка (ж)	Južna Amerika

| Antarctica | **Антарктик** (м) | Antarktik |
| the Arctic | **Арктик** (м) | Arktik |

76. Cardinal directions

north	**север** (м)	sever
to the north	**према северу**	prema severu
in the north	**на северу**	na severu
northern (adj)	**северни**	severni

south	**југ** (м)	jug
to the south	**према југу**	prema jugu
in the south	**на југу**	na jugu
southern (adj)	**јужни**	južni

west	**запад** (м)	zapad
to the west	**према западу**	prema zapadu
in the west	**на западу**	na zapadu
western (adj)	**западни**	zapadni

east	**исток** (м)	istok
to the east	**према истоку**	prema istoku
in the east	**на истоку**	na istoku
eastern (adj)	**источни**	istočni

77. Sea. Ocean

sea	**море** (с)	more
ocean	**океан** (м)	okean
gulf (bay)	**залив** (м)	zaliv
straits	**мореуз** (м)	moreuz

land (solid ground)	**копно** (с)	kopno
continent (mainland)	**континент** (м)	kontinent
island	**острво** (с)	ostrvo
peninsula	**полуострво** (с)	poluostrvo
archipelago	**архипелаг** (м)	arhipelag

bay, cove	**залив** (м)	zaliv
harbor	**лука** (ж)	luka
lagoon	**лагуна** (ж)	laguna
cape	**рт** (м)	rt

atoll	**атол** (м)	atol
reef	**гребен** (м)	greben
coral	**корал** (м)	koral
coral reef	**корални гребен** (м)	koralni greben
deep (adj)	**дубок**	dubok

depth (deep water)	дубина (ж)	dubina
abyss	бездан (м)	bezdan
trench (e.g., Mariana ~)	ров (м)	rov

| current (Ocean ~) | струја (ж) | struja |
| to surround (bathe) | окруживати | okruživati |

| shore | обала (ж) | obala |
| coast | приморје (с) | primorje |

flow (flood tide)	плима (ж)	plima
ebb (ebb tide)	осека (ж)	oseka
shoal	плићак (м)	plićak
bottom (~ of the sea)	дно (с)	dno

wave	талас (м)	talas
crest (~ of a wave)	гребен (м) таласа	greben talasa
spume (sea foam)	пена (ж)	pena

storm (sea storm)	морска олуја (ж)	morska oluja
hurricane	ураган (м)	uragan
tsunami	цунами (м)	cunami
calm (dead ~)	безветрица (ж)	bezvetrica
quiet, calm (adj)	миран	miran

| pole | пол (м) | pol |
| polar (adj) | поларни | polarni |

latitude	ширина (ж)	širina
longitude	дужина (ж)	dužina
parallel	паралела (ж)	paralela
equator	екватор (м)	ekvator

sky	небо (с)	nebo
horizon	хоризонт (м)	horizont
air	ваздух (м)	vazduh

lighthouse	светионик (м)	svetionik
to dive (vi)	ронити	roniti
to sink (ab. boat)	потонути	potonuti
treasures	благо (с)	blago

78. Seas' and Oceans' names

Atlantic Ocean	Атлантски океан (м)	Atlantski okean
Indian Ocean	Индијски океан (м)	Indijski okean
Pacific Ocean	Тихи океан (м)	Tihi okean
Arctic Ocean	Северни Ледени океан (м)	Severni Ledeni okean
Black Sea	Црно море (с)	Crno more

Red Sea	Црвено море (c)	Crveno more
Yellow Sea	Жуто море (c)	Žuto more
White Sea	Бело море (c)	Belo more
Caspian Sea	Каспијско море (c)	Kaspijsko more
Dead Sea	Мртво море (c)	Mrtvo more
Mediterranean Sea	Средоземно море (c)	Sredozemno more
Aegean Sea	Егејско море (c)	Egejsko more
Adriatic Sea	Јадранско море (c)	Jadransko more
Arabian Sea	Арабијско море (c)	Arabijsko more
Sea of Japan	Јапанско море (c)	Japansko more
Bering Sea	Берингово море (c)	Beringovo more
South China Sea	Јужно кинеско море (c)	Južno kinesko more
Coral Sea	Корално море (c)	Koralno more
Tasman Sea	Тасманово море (c)	Tasmanovo more
Caribbean Sea	Карипско море (c)	Karipsko more
Barents Sea	Баренцово море (c)	Barencovo more
Kara Sea	Карско море (c)	Karsko more
North Sea	Северно море (c)	Severno more
Baltic Sea	Балтичко море (c)	Baltičko more
Norwegian Sea	Норвешко море (c)	Norveško more

79. Mountains

mountain	планина (ж)	planina
mountain range	планински венац (м)	planinski venac
mountain ridge	планински гребен (м)	planinski greben
summit, top	врх (м)	vrh
peak	планиски врх (м)	planiski vrh
foot (~ of the mountain)	подножје (c)	podnožje
slope (mountainside)	нагиб (м)	nagib
volcano	вулкан (м)	vulkan
active volcano	активан вулкан (м)	aktivan vulkan
dormant volcano	угашени вулкан (м)	ugašeni vulkan
eruption	ерупција (ж)	erupcija
crater	кратер (м)	krater
magma	магма (ж)	magma
lava	лава (ж)	lava
molten (~ lava)	усијан	usijan
canyon	кањон (м)	kanjon
gorge	клисура (ж)	klisura

| crevice | пукотина (ж) | pukotina |
| abyss (chasm) | амбис (м), понор (м) | ambis, ponor |

pass, col	превој (м)	prevoj
plateau	плато (с)	plato
cliff	литица (ж)	litica
hill	брег (м)	breg

glacier	леденик (м)	ledenik
waterfall	водопад (м)	vodopad
geyser	гејзер (м)	gejzer
lake	језеро (с)	jezero

plain	равница (ж)	ravnica
landscape	пејзаж (м)	pejzaž
echo	одјек (м)	odjek

alpinist	алпиниста (м)	alpinista
rock climber	алпиниста (м)	alpinista
to conquer (in climbing)	освајати	osvajati
climb (an easy ~)	пењање (с)	penjanje

80. Mountains names

The Alps	Алпи (м мн)	Alpi
Mont Blanc	Монблан (м)	Monblan
The Pyrenees	Пиринеји (м мн)	Pirineji

The Carpathians	Карпати (м мн)	Karpati
The Ural Mountains	Урал (м)	Ural
The Caucasus Mountains	Кавказ (м)	Kavkaz
Mount Elbrus	Елбрус (м)	Elbrus

The Altai Mountains	Алтај (м)	Altaj
The Tian Shan	Тјен Шан (м)	Tjen Šan
The Pamir Mountains	Памир (м)	Pamir
The Himalayas	Хималаји (м мн)	Himalaji
Mount Everest	Монт Еверест (м)	Mont Everest

| The Andes | Анди (м мн) | Andi |
| Mount Kilimanjaro | Килиманџаро (с) | Kilimandžaro |

81. Rivers

river	река (ж)	reka
spring (natural source)	извор (м)	izvor
riverbed (river channel)	корито (с)	korito
basin (river valley)	слив (м)	sliv

to flow into …	уливати се (ж)	ulivati se
tributary	притока (ж)	pritoka
bank (of river)	обала (ж)	obala

current (stream)	ток (м)	tok
downstream (adv)	низводно	nizvodno
upstream (adv)	узводно	uzvodno

inundation	поплава (ж)	poplava
flooding	поводањ (м)	povodanj
to overflow (vi)	изливати се	izlivati se
to flood (vt)	поплавити	poplaviti

| shallow (shoal) | плићак (м) | plićak |
| rapids | брзаци (м мн) | brzaci |

dam	брана (ж)	brana
canal	канал (м)	kanal
reservoir (artificial lake)	вештачко језеро (с)	veštačko jezero
sluice, lock	устава (ж)	ustava

water body (pond, etc.)	резервоар (м)	rezervoar
swamp (marshland)	мочвара (ж)	močvara
bog, marsh	баруштина (ж)	baruština
whirlpool	вртлог (м)	vrtlog

stream (brook)	поток (м)	potok
drinking (ab. water)	питка	pitka
fresh (~ water)	слатка (вода)	slatka (voda)

| ice | лед (м) | led |
| to freeze over (ab. river, etc.) | смрзнути се | smrznuti se |

82. Rivers' names

| Seine | Сена (ж) | Sena |
| Loire | Лоара (ж) | Loara |

Thames	Темза (ж)	Temza
Rhine	Рајна (ж)	Rajna
Danube	Дунав (м)	Dunav

Volga	Волга (ж)	Volga
Don	Дон (м)	Don
Lena	Лена (ж)	Lena

Yellow River	Хуангхе (ж)	Huanghe
Yangtze	Јангцекјанг (м)	Jangcekjang
Mekong	Меконг (м)	Mekong

Ganges	Ганг (м)	Gang
Nile River	Нил (м)	Nil
Congo River	Конго (ж)	Kongo
Okavango River	Окаванго (ж)	Okavango
Zambezi River	Замбези (ж)	Zambezi
Limpopo River	Лимпопо (ж)	Limpopo
Mississippi River	Мисисипи (ж)	Misisipi

83. Forest

| forest, wood | шума (ж) | šuma |
| forest (as adj) | шумски | šumski |

thick forest	честар (м)	čestar
grove	шумарак (м)	šumarak
forest clearing	пропланак (м)	proplanak

| thicket | шипраг (м) | šiprag |
| scrubland | шипражје (с) | šipražje |

| footpath (troddenpath) | стаза (ж) | staza |
| gully | јаруга (ж) | jaruga |

tree	дрво (с)	drvo
leaf	лист (м)	list
leaves (foliage)	лишће (с)	lišće

fall of leaves	листопад (м)	listopad
to fall (ab. leaves)	опадати	opadati
top (of the tree)	врх (м)	vrh

branch	грана (ж)	grana
bough	чвор (м)	čvor
bud (on shrub, tree)	пупољак (м)	pupoljak
needle (of pine tree)	иглица (ж)	iglica
pine cone	шишарка (ж)	šišarka

hollow (in a tree)	дупља (ж)	duplja
nest	гнездо (с)	gnezdo
burrow (animal hole)	јазбина (ж), рупа (ж)	jazbina, rupa

trunk	стабло (с)	stablo
root	корен (м)	koren
bark	кора (ж)	kora
moss	маховина (ж)	mahovina

to uproot (remove trees or tree stumps)	крчити	krčiti
to chop down	сећи	seći
to deforest (vt)	крчити шуму	krčiti šumu

tree stump	пањ (м)	panj
campfire	логорска ватра (ж)	logorska vatra
forest fire	шумски пожар (м)	šumski požar
to extinguish (vt)	гасити	gasiti

forest ranger	шумар (м)	šumar
protection	заштита (ж)	zaštita
to protect (~ nature)	штитити	štititi
poacher	ловокрадица (м)	lovokradica
steel trap	клопка (ж)	klopka

| to gather, to pick (vt) | брати | brati |
| to lose one's way | залутати | zalutati |

84. Natural resources

natural resources	природна богатства (с мн)	prirodna bogatstva
minerals	руде (с мн)	rude
deposits	лежишта (с мн)	ležišta
field (e.g., oilfield)	налазиште (с)	nalazište

to mine (extract)	рударити	rudariti
mining (extraction)	рударство (с)	rudarstvo
ore	руда (ж)	ruda
mine (e.g., for coal)	рудник (м)	rudnik
shaft (mine ~)	рударско окно (с)	rudarsko okno
miner	рудар (м)	rudar

| gas (natural ~) | плин (м) | plin |
| gas pipeline | плиновод (м) | plinovod |

oil (petroleum)	нафта (ж)	nafta
oil pipeline	нафтовод (м)	naftovod
oil well	нафтна бушотина (ж)	naftna bušotina
derrick (tower)	нафтна платформа (ж)	naftna platforma
tanker	танкер (м)	tanker

sand	песак (м)	pesak
limestone	кречњак (м)	krečnjak
gravel	шљунак (м)	šljunak
peat	тресет (м)	treset
clay	глина (ж)	glina
coal	угаљ (м)	ugalj

iron (ore)	гвожђе (с)	gvožđe
gold	злато (с)	zlato
silver	сребро (с)	srebro
nickel	никл (м)	nikl
copper	бакар (м)	bakar

zinc	цинк (м)	cink
manganese	манган (м)	mangan
mercury	жива (ж)	živa
lead	олово (с)	olovo

mineral	минерал (м)	mineral
crystal	кристал (м)	kristal
marble	мермер (м)	mermer
uranium	уран (м)	uran

85. Weather

weather	време (с)	vreme
weather forecast	временска прогноза (ж)	vremenska prognoza
temperature	температура (ж)	temperatura
thermometer	термометар (м)	termometar
barometer	барометар (м)	barometar

humid (adj)	влажан	vlažan
humidity	влажност (ж)	vlažnost
heat (extreme ~)	врућина (ж)	vrućina
hot (torrid)	врућ	vruć
it's hot	вруће је	vruće je

| it's warm | топло је | toplo je |
| warm (moderately hot) | топао | topao |

| it's cold | хладно је | hladno je |
| cold (adj) | хладан | hladan |

sun	сунце (с)	sunce
to shine (vi)	сијати	sijati
sunny (day)	сунчан	sunčan
to come up (vi)	изаћи	izaći
to set (vi)	заћи	zaći

cloud	облак (м)	oblak
cloudy (adj)	облачан	oblačan
rain cloud	кишни облак (м)	kišni oblak
somber (gloomy)	тмуран	tmuran

rain	киша (ж)	kiša
it's raining	пада киша	pada kiša
rainy (~ day, weather)	кишовит	kišovit
to drizzle (vi)	сипити	sipiti

pouring rain	јака киша (ж)	jaka kiša
downpour	пљусак (м)	pljusak
heavy (e.g., ~ rain)	јак	jak
puddle	бара (ж)	bara

to get wet (in rain)	покиснути	pokisnuti
fog (mist)	магла (ж)	magla
foggy	магловит	maglovit
snow	снег (м)	sneg
it's snowing	пада снег	pada sneg

86. Severe weather. Natural disasters

thunderstorm	олуја (ж)	oluja
lightning (~ strike)	муња (ж)	munja
to flash (vi)	севати	sevati

thunder	гром (м)	grom
to thunder (vi)	грмети	grmeti
it's thundering	грми	grmi

hail	град (м)	grad
it's hailing	пада град	pada grad

to flood (vt)	поплавити	poplaviti
flood, inundation	поплава (ж)	poplava

earthquake	земљотрес (м)	zemljotres
tremor, quake	потрес (м)	potres
epicenter	епицентар (м)	epicentar

eruption	ерупција (ж)	erupcija
lava	лава (ж)	lava

twister	пијавица (ж)	pijavica
tornado	торнадо (м)	tornado
typhoon	тајфун (м)	tajfun

hurricane	ураган (м)	uragan
storm	олуја (ж)	oluja
tsunami	цунами (м)	cunami

cyclone	циклон (м)	ciklon
bad weather	невреме (с)	nevreme
fire (accident)	пожар (м)	požar
disaster	катастрофа (ж)	katastrofa
meteorite	метеорит (м)	meteorit

avalanche	лавина (ж)	lavina
snowslide	усов (м)	usov
blizzard	мећава (ж)	mećava
snowstorm	вејавица (ж)	vejavica

FAUNA

T&P Books Publishing

87. Mammals. Predators

predator	грабљивац (м)	grabljivac
tiger	тигар (м)	tigar
lion	лав (м)	lav
wolf	вук (м)	vuk
fox	лисица (ж)	lisica
jaguar	јагуар (м)	jaguar
leopard	леопард (м)	leopard
cheetah	гепард (м)	gepard
black panther	пантер (м)	panter
puma	пума (ж)	puma
snow leopard	снежни леопард (м)	snežni leopard
lynx	рис (м)	ris
coyote	којот (м)	kojot
jackal	шакал (м)	šakal
hyena	хијена (ж)	hijena

88. Wild animals

animal	животиња (ж)	životinja
beast (animal)	зверка (ж)	zverka
squirrel	веверица (ж)	veverica
hedgehog	јеж (м)	jež
hare	зец (м)	zec
rabbit	кунић (м)	kunić
badger	јазавац (м)	jazavac
raccoon	ракун (м)	rakun
hamster	хрчак (м)	hrčak
marmot	мрмот (м)	mrmot
mole	кртица (ж)	krtica
mouse	миш (м)	miš
rat	пацов (м)	pacov
bat	слепи миш (м)	slepi miš
ermine	хермелин (м)	hermelin
sable	самур (м)	samur
marten	куна (ж)	kuna

weasel	ласица (ж)	lasica
mink	нерц (м)	nerc
beaver	дабар (м)	dabar
otter	видра (ж)	vidra
horse	коњ (м)	konj
moose	лос (м)	los
deer	јелен (м)	jelen
camel	камила (ж)	kamila
bison	бизон (м)	bizon
aurochs	зубар (м)	zubar
buffalo	бивол (м)	bivol
zebra	зебра (ж)	zebra
antelope	антилопа (ж)	antilopa
roe deer	срна (ж)	srna
fallow deer	јелен лопатар (м)	jelen lopatar
chamois	дивокоза (ж)	divokoza
wild boar	дивља свиња (ж), вепар (м)	divlja svinja, vepar
whale	кит (м)	kit
seal	фока (ж)	foka
walrus	морж (м)	morž
fur seal	северна фока (ж)	severna foka
dolphin	делфин (м)	delfin
bear	медвед (м)	medved
polar bear	бели медвед (м)	beli medved
panda	панда (ж)	panda
monkey	мајмун (м)	majmun
chimpanzee	шимпанза (ж)	šimpanza
orangutan	орангутан (м)	orangutan
gorilla	горила (ж)	gorila
macaque	макаки (м)	makaki
gibbon	гибон (м)	gibon
elephant	слон (м)	slon
rhinoceros	носорог (м)	nosorog
giraffe	жирафа (ж)	žirafa
hippopotamus	нилски коњ (м)	nilski konj
kangaroo	кенгур (м)	kengur
koala (bear)	коала (ж)	koala
mongoose	мунгос (м)	mungos
chinchilla	чинчила (ж)	činčila
skunk	твор (м)	tvor
porcupine	дикобраз (м)	dikobraz

89. Domestic animals

cat	мачка (ж)	mačka
tomcat	мачак (м)	mačak
dog	пас (м)	pas
horse	коњ (м)	konj
stallion (male horse)	ждребац (м)	ždrebac
mare	кобила (ж)	kobila
cow	крава (ж)	krava
bull	бик (м)	bik
ox	во (м)	vo
sheep (ewe)	овца (ж)	ovca
ram	ован (м)	ovan
goat	коза (ж)	koza
billy goat, he-goat	јарац (м)	jarac
donkey	магарац (м)	magarac
mule	мазга (ж)	mazga
pig, hog	свиња (ж)	svinja
piglet	прасе (с)	prase
rabbit	кунић, домаћи зец (м)	kunić, domaći zec
hen (chicken)	кокош (ж)	kokoš
rooster	певац (м)	pevac
duck	патка (ж)	patka
drake	патак (м)	patak
goose	гуска (ж)	guska
tom turkey, gobbler	ћуран (м)	ćuran
turkey (hen)	ћурка (ж)	ćurka
domestic animals	домаће животиње (ж мн)	domaće životinje
tame (e.g., ~ hamster)	питом	pitom
to tame (vt)	припитомљавати	pripitomljavati
to breed (vt)	узгајати	uzgajati
farm	фарма (ж)	farma
poultry	живина (ж)	živina
cattle	стока (ж)	stoka
herd (cattle)	стадо (с)	stado
stable	штала (ж)	štala
pigpen	свињац (м)	svinjac
cowshed	стаја (ж)	staja
rabbit hutch	зечињак (м)	zečinjak
hen house	кокошињац (м)	kokošinjac

90. Birds

bird	птица (ж)	ptica
pigeon	голуб (м)	golub
sparrow	врабац (м)	vrabac
tit (great tit)	сеница (ж)	senica
magpie	сврака (ж)	svraka

raven	гавран (м)	gavran
crow	врана (ж)	vrana
jackdaw	чавка (ж)	čavka
rook	гачац (м)	gačac

duck	патка (ж)	patka
goose	гуска (ж)	guska
pheasant	фазан (м)	fazan

eagle	орао (м)	orao
hawk	јастреб (м)	jastreb
falcon	соко (м)	soko
vulture	суп (м)	sup
condor (Andean ~)	кондор (м)	kondor

swan	лабуд (м)	labud
crane	ждрал (м)	ždral
stork	рода (ж)	roda

parrot	папагај (м)	papagaj
hummingbird	колибри (ж)	kolibri
peacock	паун (м)	paun

ostrich	ној (м)	noj
heron	чапља (ж)	čaplja
flamingo	фламинго (м)	flamingo
pelican	пеликан (м)	pelikan

| nightingale | славуј (м) | slavuj |
| swallow | ластавица (ж) | lastavica |

thrush	дрозд (м)	drozd
song thrush	дрозд певач (м)	drozd pevač
blackbird	кос (м)	kos

swift	брегуница (ж)	bregunica
lark	шева (ж)	ševa
quail	препелица (ж)	prepelica

woodpecker	детлић (м)	detlić
cuckoo	кукавица (ж)	kukavica
owl	сова (ж)	sova
eagle owl	совуљага (ж)	sovuljaga

wood grouse	велики тетреб (м)	veliki tetreb
black grouse	мали тетреб (м)	mali tetreb
partridge	јаребица (ж)	jarebica

starling	чворак (м)	čvorak
canary	канаринац (м)	kanarinac
hazel grouse	лештарка (ж)	leštarka
chaffinch	зеба (ж)	zeba
bullfinch	зимовка (ж)	zimovka

seagull	галеб (м)	galeb
albatross	албатрос (м)	albatros
penguin	пингвин (м)	pingvin

91. Fish. Marine animals

bream	деверика (ж)	deverika
carp	шаран (м)	šaran
perch	гргеч (м)	grgeč
catfish	сом (м)	som
pike	штука (ж)	štuka

| salmon | лосос (м) | losos |
| sturgeon | јесетра (ж) | jesetra |

herring	харинга (ж)	haringa
Atlantic salmon	атлантски лосос (м)	atlantski losos
mackerel	скуша (ж)	skuša
flatfish	риба-лист (ж)	riba-list

zander, pike perch	смуђ (м)	smuđ
cod	бакалар (м)	bakalar
tuna	туњ (м)	tunj
trout	пастрмка (ж)	pastrmka

eel	јегуља (ж)	jegulja
electric ray	трновка (ж)	trnovka
moray eel	мурина (ж)	murina
piranha	пирана (ж)	pirana

shark	ајкула (ж)	ajkula
dolphin	делфин (м)	delfin
whale	кит (м)	kit

crab	морски рак (м)	morski rak
jellyfish	медуза (ж)	meduza
octopus	хоботница (ж)	hobotnica

| starfish | морска звезда (ж) | morska zvezda |
| sea urchin | морски јеж (м) | morski jež |

seahorse	морски коњић (м)	morski konjić
oyster	острига (ж)	ostriga
shrimp	морски рачић (м)	morski račić
lobster	хлап (м)	hlap
spiny lobster	лангуст, јастог (м)	langust, jastog

92. Amphibians. Reptiles

| snake | змија (ж) | zmija |
| venomous (snake) | отрован | otrovan |

viper	поскок (м)	poskok
cobra	кобра (ж)	kobra
python	питон (м)	piton
boa	удав (м)	udav

grass snake	белоушка (ж)	belouška
rattle snake	звечарка (ж)	zvečarka
anaconda	анаконда (ж)	anakonda

lizard	гуштер (м)	gušter
iguana	игуана (ж)	iguana
monitor lizard	варан (м)	varan
salamander	даждевњак (м)	daždevnjak
chameleon	камелеон (м)	kameleon
scorpion	шкорпија (ж)	škorpija

turtle	корњача (ж)	kornjača
frog	жаба (ж)	žaba
toad	крастача (ж)	krastača
crocodile	крокодил (м)	krokodil

93. Insects

insect, bug	инсект (м)	insekt
butterfly	лептир (м)	leptir
ant	мрав (м)	mrav
fly	мува (ж)	muva
mosquito	комарац (м)	komarac
beetle	буба (ж)	buba

wasp	оса (ж)	osa
bee	пчела (ж)	pčela
bumblebee	бумбар (м)	bumbar
gadfly (botfly)	обад (м)	obad

| spider | паук (м) | pauk |
| spiderweb | паучина (ж) | paučina |

dragonfly	**вилин коњиц** (м)	vilin konjic
grasshopper	**скакавац** (м)	skakavac
moth (night butterfly)	**лептирица** (ж)	leptirica
cockroach	**бубашваба** (ж)	bubašvaba
tick	**крпељ** (м)	krpelj
flea	**бува** (ж)	buva
midge	**мушица** (ж)	mušica
locust	**миграторни скакавац** (м)	migratorni skakavac
snail	**пуж** (м)	puž
cricket	**цврчак** (м)	cvrčak
lightning bug	**свитац** (м)	svitac
ladybug	**бубамара** (ж)	bubamara
cockchafer	**гундељ** (м)	gundelj
leech	**пијавица** (ж)	pijavica
caterpillar	**гусеница** (ж)	gusenica
earthworm	**црв** (м)	crv
larva	**ларва** (ж)	larva

FLORA

T&P Books Publishing

94. Trees

tree	дрво (с)	drvo
deciduous (adj)	листопадно	listopadno
coniferous (adj)	четинарско	četinarsko
evergreen (adj)	зимзелено	zimzeleno
apple tree	јабука (ж)	jabuka
pear tree	крушка (ж)	kruška
sweet cherry tree	трешња (ж)	trešnja
sour cherry tree	вишња (ж)	višnja
plum tree	шљива (ж)	šljiva
birch	бреза (ж)	breza
oak	храст (м)	hrast
linden tree	липа (ж)	lipa
aspen	јасика (ж)	jasika
maple	јавор (м)	javor
spruce	јела (ж)	jela
pine	бор (м)	bor
larch	ариш (м)	ariš
fir tree	јела (ж)	jela
cedar	кедар (м)	kedar
poplar	топола (ж)	topola
rowan	оскоруша (ж)	oskoruša
willow	врба (ж)	vrba
alder	јова (ж)	jova
beech	буква (ж)	bukva
elm	брест (м)	brest
ash (tree)	јасен (м)	jasen
chestnut	кестен (м)	kesten
magnolia	магнолија (ж)	magnolija
palm tree	палма (ж)	palma
cypress	чемпрес (м)	čempres
mangrove	мангров (м)	mangrov
baobab	баобаб (м)	baobab
eucalyptus	еукалиптус (м)	eukaliptus
sequoia	секвоја (ж)	sekvoja

95. Shrubs

| bush | грм (м) | grm |
| shrub | жбун (м) | žbun |

| grapevine | винова лоза (ж) | vinova loza |
| vineyard | виноград (м) | vinograd |

raspberry bush	малина (ж)	malina
blackcurrant bush	црна рибизла (ж)	crna ribizla
redcurrant bush	црвена рибизла (ж)	crvena ribizla
gooseberry bush	огрозд (м)	ogrozd

acacia	багрем (м)	bagrem
barberry	жутика, шимширика (ж)	žutika, šimširika
jasmine	јасмин (м)	jasmin

juniper	клека (ж)	kleka
rosebush	ружа (ж)	ruža
dog rose	шипак (м)	šipak

96. Fruits. Berries

fruit	воћка (ж)	voćka
fruits	воће (с мн)	voće
apple	јабука (ж)	jabuka
pear	крушка (ж)	kruška
plum	шљива (ж)	šljiva

strawberry (garden ~)	јагода (ж)	jagoda
sour cherry	вишња (ж)	višnja
sweet cherry	трешња (ж)	trešnja
grape	грожђе (с)	grožđe

raspberry	малина (ж)	malina
blackcurrant	црна рибизла (ж)	crna ribizla
redcurrant	црвена рибизла (ж)	crvena ribizla
gooseberry	огрозд (м)	ogrozd
cranberry	маховница (ж)	mahovnica

orange	поморанџа (ж)	pomorandža
mandarin	мандарина (ж)	mandarina
pineapple	ананас (м)	ananas
banana	банана (ж)	banana
date	урма (ж)	urma

lemon	лимун (м)	limun
apricot	кајсија (ж)	kajsija
peach	бресква (ж)	breskva

| kiwi | киви (м) | kivi |
| grapefruit | грејпфрут (м) | grejpfrut |

berry	бобица (ж)	bobica
berries	бобице (ж мн)	bobice
cowberry	брусница (ж)	brusnica
wild strawberry	шумска јагода (ж)	šumska jagoda
bilberry	боровница (ж)	borovnica

97. Flowers. Plants

| flower | цвет (м) | cvet |
| bouquet (of flowers) | букет (ж) | buket |

rose (flower)	ружа (ж)	ruža
tulip	лала (ж), тулипан (м)	lala, tulipan
carnation	каранфил (м)	karanfil
gladiolus	гладиола (ж)	gladiola

cornflower	различак (м)	različak
harebell	звонце (с)	zvonce
dandelion	маслачак (м)	maslačak
camomile	камилица (ж)	kamilica

aloe	алоја (ж)	aloja
cactus	кактус (м)	kaktus
rubber plant, ficus	фикус (м)	fikus

lily	љиљан (м)	ljiljan
geranium	здравац (м)	zdravac
hyacinth	зумбул (м)	zumbul

mimosa	мимоза (ж)	mimoza
narcissus	нарцис (м)	narcis
nasturtium	драгољуб (м)	dragoljub

orchid	орхидеја (ж)	orhideja
peony	божур (м)	božur
violet	љубичица (ж)	ljubičica

pansy	дан и ноћ (м)	dan i noć
forget-me-not	споменак (м)	spomenak
daisy	бела рада (ж), красуљак (м)	bela rada, krasuljak

poppy	мак (м)	mak
hemp	конопља (ж)	konoplja
mint	нана (ж), метвица (ж)	nana, metvica
lily of the valley	ђурђевак (м)	đurđevak
snowdrop	висибаба (ж)	visibaba

nettle	коприва (ж)	kopriva
sorrel	кисељак (м)	kiseljak
water lily	локвањ (м)	lokvanj
fern	папрат (м)	paprat
lichen	лишај (м)	lišaj

greenhouse (tropical ~)	стаклена башта (ж)	staklena bašta
lawn	травњак (м)	travnjak
flowerbed	цветна леја (ж)	cvetna leja

plant	биљка (ж)	biljka
grass	трава (ж)	trava
blade of grass	травчица (ж)	travčica

leaf	лист (м)	list
petal	латица (ж)	latica
stem	стабло (с)	stablo
tuber	кртола (ж)	krtola

young plant (shoot)	изданак (м)	izdanak
thorn	трн (м)	trn

to blossom (vi)	цветати	cvetati
to fade, to wither	венути	venuti
smell (odor)	мирис (м)	miris
to cut (flowers)	одсећи	odseći
to pick (a flower)	убрати	ubrati

98. Cereals, grains

grain	зрно (с)	zrno
cereal crops	житарице (ж мн)	žitarice
ear (of barley, etc.)	клас (м)	klas

wheat	пшеница (ж)	pšenica
rye	раж (ж)	raž
oats	овас (м)	ovas

millet	просо (с)	proso
barley	јечам (м)	ječam

corn	кукуруз (м)	kukuruz
rice	пиринач (м)	pirinač
buckwheat	хељда (ж)	heljda

pea plant	грашак (м)	grašak
kidney bean	пасуљ (м)	pasulj
soy	соја (ж)	soja
lentil	сочиво (с)	sočivo
beans (pulse crops)	махунарке (ж мн)	mahunarke

COUNTRIES OF
THE WORLD

T&P Books Publishing

99. Countries. Part 1

Afghanistan	Авганистан (м)	Avganistan
Albania	Албанија (ж)	Albanija
Argentina	Аргентина (ж)	Argentina
Armenia	Јерменија (ж)	Jermenija
Australia	Аустралија (ж)	Australija
Austria	Аустрија (ж)	Austrija
Azerbaijan	Азербејџан (м)	Azerbejdžan

The Bahamas	Бахами (с мн)	Bahami
Bangladesh	Бангладеш (м)	Bangladeš
Belarus	Белорусија (ж)	Belorusija
Belgium	Белгија (ж)	Belgija
Bolivia	Боливија (ж)	Bolivija
Bosnia and Herzegovina	Босна и Херцеговина (ж)	Bosna i Hercegovina
Brazil	Бразил (м)	Brazil
Bulgaria	Бугарска (ж)	Bugarska

Cambodia	Камбоџа (ж)	Kambodža
Canada	Канада (ж)	Kanada
Chile	Чиле (м)	Čile
China	Кина (ж)	Kina
Colombia	Колумбија (ж)	Kolumbija
Croatia	Хрвастка (ж)	Hrvastka
Cuba	Куба (ж)	Kuba
Cyprus	Кипар (м)	Kipar
Czech Republic	Чешка република (ж)	Češka republika

Denmark	Данска (ж)	Danska
Dominican Republic	Доминиканска република (ж)	Dominikanska republika
Ecuador	Еквадор (м)	Ekvador
Egypt	Египат (м)	Egipat
England	Енглеска (ж)	Engleska
Estonia	Естонија (ж)	Estonija
Finland	Финска (ж)	Finska
France	Француска (ж)	Francuska
French Polynesia	Француска Полинезија (ж)	Francuska Polinezija

Georgia	Грузија (ж)	Gruzija
Germany	Немачка (ж)	Nemačka
Ghana	Гана (ж)	Gana
Great Britain	Велика Британија (ж)	Velika Britanija
Greece	Грчка (ж)	Grčka

| Haiti | **Хаити** (м) | Haiti |
| Hungary | **Мађарска** (ж) | Mađarska |

100. Countries. Part 2

Iceland	**Исланд** (м)	Island
India	**Индија** (ж)	Indija
Indonesia	**Индонезија** (ж)	Indonezija
Iran	**Иран** (м)	Iran
Iraq	**Ирак** (м)	Irak
Ireland	**Ирска** (ж)	Irska
Israel	**Израел** (м)	Izrael
Italy	**Италија** (ж)	Italija

Jamaica	**Јамајка** (ж)	Jamajka
Japan	**Јапан** (м)	Japan
Jordan	**Јордан** (м)	Jordan
Kazakhstan	**Казахстан** (м)	Kazahstan
Kenya	**Кенија** (ж)	Kenija
Kirghizia	**Киргистан** (м)	Kirgistan
Kuwait	**Кувајт** (м)	Kuvajt

Laos	**Лаос** (м)	Laos
Latvia	**Летонија** (ж)	Letonija
Lebanon	**Либан** (м)	Liban
Libya	**Либија** (ж)	Libija
Liechtenstein	**Лихтенштајн** (м)	Lihtenštajn
Lithuania	**Литванија** (ж)	Litvanija
Luxembourg	**Луксембург** (м)	Luksemburg

Macedonia (Republic of ~)	**Македонија** (ж)	Makedonija
Madagascar	**Мадагаскар** (м)	Madagaskar
Malaysia	**Малејзија** (ж)	Malejzija
Malta	**Малта** (ж)	Malta
Mexico	**Мексико** (м)	Meksiko
Moldova, Moldavia	**Молдавија** (ж)	Moldavija

Monaco	**Монако** (м)	Monako
Mongolia	**Монголија** (ж)	Mongolija
Montenegro	**Црна Гора** (ж)	Crna Gora

| Morocco | **Мароко** (м) | Maroko |
| Myanmar | **Мијанмар** (м) | Mijanmar |

Namibia	**Намибија** (ж)	Namibija
Nepal	**Непал** (м)	Nepal
Netherlands	**Холандија** (ж)	Holandija
New Zealand	**Нови Зеланд** (м)	Novi Zeland
North Korea	**Северна Кореја** (ж)	Severna Koreja
Norway	**Норвешка** (ж)	Norveška

101. Countries. Part 3

Pakistan	Пакистан (м)	Pakistan
Palestine	Палестина (ж)	Palestina
Panama	Панама (ж)	Panama
Paraguay	Парагвај (м)	Paragvaj
Peru	Перу (м)	Peru
Poland	Пољска (ж)	Poljska
Portugal	Португалија (ж)	Portugalija
Romania	Румунија (ж)	Rumunija
Russia	Русија (ж)	Rusija

Saudi Arabia	Саудијска Арабија (ж)	Saudijska Arabija
Scotland	Шкотска (ж)	Škotska
Senegal	Сенегал (м)	Senegal
Serbia	Србија (ж)	Srbija
Slovakia	Словачка (ж)	Slovačka
Slovenia	Словенија (ж)	Slovenija

South Africa	Јужноафричка република (ж)	Južnoafrička republika
South Korea	Јужна Кореја (ж)	Južna Koreja
Spain	Шпанија (ж)	Španija
Suriname	Суринам (м)	Surinam
Sweden	Шведска (ж)	Švedska
Switzerland	Швајцарска (ж)	Švajcarska
Syria	Сирија (ж)	Sirija

Taiwan	Тајван (м)	Tajvan
Tajikistan	Тациикистан (м)	Tadžikistan
Tanzania	Танзанија (ж)	Tanzanija
Tasmania	Тасманија (ж)	Tasmanija
Thailand	Тајланд (м)	Tajland
Tunisia	Тунис (м)	Tunis
Turkey	Турска (ж)	Turska
Turkmenistan	Туркменистан (м)	Turkmenistan

Ukraine	Украјина (ж)	Ukrajina
United Arab Emirates	Уједињени Арапски Емирати (м мн)	Ujedinjeni Arapski Emirati
United States of America	Сједињене Америчке Државе (ж мн)	Sjedinjene Američke Države
Uruguay	Уругвај (м)	Urugvaj
Uzbekistan	Узбекистан (м)	Uzbekistan

Vatican	Ватикан (м)	Vatikan
Venezuela	Венецуела (ж)	Venecuela
Vietnam	Вијетнам (м)	Vijetnam
Zanzibar	Занзибар (м)	Zanzibar

GASTRONOMIC GLOSSARY

This section contains a lot of
words and terms associated
with food. This dictionary will
make it easier for you to
understand the menu at a
restaurant and choose
the right dish

T&P Books Publishing

English-Serbian gastronomic glossary

aftertaste	паукус (м)	paukus
almond	бадем (м)	badem
anise	анис (м)	anis
aperitif	аперитив (м)	aperitiv
appetite	апетит (м)	apetit
appetizer	предјело (с)	predjelo
apple	јабука (ж)	jabuka
apricot	кајсија (ж)	kajsija
artichoke	артичока (ж)	artičoka
asparagus	шпаргла (ж)	špargla
Atlantic salmon	атлантски лосос (м)	atlantski losos
avocado	авокадо (м)	avokado
bacon	сланина (ж)	slanina
banana	банана (ж)	banana
barley	јечам (м)	ječam
bartender	бармен (м)	barmen
basil	босиљак (м)	bosiljak
bay leaf	ловор (м)	lovor
beans	махунарке (ж мн)	mahunarke
beef	говедина (ж)	govedina
beer	пиво (с)	pivo
beetroot	цвекла (ж)	cvekla
bell pepper	паприка (ж)	paprika
berries	бобице (ж мн)	bobice
berry	бобица (ж)	bobica
bilberry	боровница (ж)	borovnica
birch bolete	брезов дед (м)	brezov ded
bitter	горак	gorak
black coffee	црна кафа (ж)	crna kafa
black pepper	црни бибер (м)	crni biber
black tea	црни чај (м)	crni čaj
blackberry	купина (ж)	kupina
blackcurrant	црна рибизла (ж)	crna ribizla
boiled	куван	kuvan
bottle opener	отварач (м)	otvarač
bread	хлеб (м)	hleb
breakfast	доручак (м)	doručak
bream	деверика (ж)	deverika
broccoli	броколи (м)	brokoli
Brussels sprouts	прокељ (м)	prokelj
buckwheat	хељда (ж)	heljda
butter	маслац (м)	maslac
buttercream	крем (м)	krem
cabbage	купус (м)	kupus

cake	колач (м)	kolač
cake	торта (ж)	torta
calorie	калорија (ж)	kalorija
can opener	отварач (м)	otvarač
candy	бомбона (ж)	bombona
canned food	конзервирана храна (ж)	konzervirana hrana
cappuccino	капућино (м)	kapućino
caraway	ким (м)	kim
carbohydrates	угљени хидрати (м мн)	ugljeni hidrati
carbonated	газирана	gazirana
carp	шаран (м)	šaran
carrot	шаргарепа (ж)	šargarepa
catfish	сом (м)	som
cauliflower	карфиол (м)	karfiol
caviar	кавијар (м)	kavijar
celery	целер (м)	celer
cep	вргањ (м)	vrganj
cereal crops	житарице (ж мн)	žitarice
cereal grains	житарице (ж мн)	žitarice
champagne	шампањац (м)	šampanjac
chanterelle	лисичарка (ж)	lisičarka
check	рачун (м)	račun
cheese	сир (м)	sir
chewing gum	гума (ж) за жвакање	guma za žvakanje
chicken	пилетина (ж)	piletina
chocolate	чоколада (ж)	čokolada
chocolate	чоколадан	čokoladan
cinnamon	цимет (м)	cimet
clear soup	буљон (м)	buljon
cloves	каранфил (м)	karanfil
cocktail	коктел (м)	koktel
coconut	кокосов орах (м)	kokosov orah
cod	бакалар (м)	bakalar
coffee	кафа (ж)	kafa
coffee with milk	кафа (ж) са млеком	kafa sa mlekom
cognac	коњак (м)	konjak
cold	хладан	hladan
condensed milk	кондензовано млеко (с)	kondenzovano mleko
condiment	додатак, зачин (м)	dodatak, začin
confectionery	посластичарски производи (м мн)	poslastičarski proizvodi
cookies	бисквити (м мн)	biskviti
coriander	кориандер (м)	koriander
corkscrew	вадичеп (м)	vadičep
corn	кукуруз (м)	kukuruz
corn	кукуруз (м)	kukuruz
cornflakes	кукурузне пахуљице (ж мн)	kukuruzne pahuljice
course, dish	јело (с)	jelo
cowberry	брусница (ж)	brusnica
crab	морски рак (м)	morski rak
cranberry	маховница (ж)	mahovnica

cream	павлака (ж)	pavlaka
crumb	мрва (ж)	mrva
crustaceans	ракови (м мн)	rakovi
cucumber	краставац (м)	krastavac
cuisine	кухиња (ж)	kuhinja
cup	шоља (ж)	šolja
dark beer	тамно пиво (с)	tamno pivo
date	урма (ж)	urma
death cap	отровна гљива (ж)	otrovna gljiva
dessert	десерт (м)	desert
diet	дијета (ж)	dijeta
dill	мирођија (ж)	mirođija
dinner	вечера (ж)	večera
dried	сушен	sušen
drinking water	вода (ж) за пиће	voda za piće
duck	патка (ж)	patka
ear	клас (м)	klas
edible mushroom	јестива печурка (ж)	jestiva pečurka
eel	јегуља (ж)	jegulja
egg	јаје (с)	jaje
egg white	беланце (с)	belance
egg yolk	жуманце (с)	žumance
eggplant	плави патлиџан (м)	plavi patlidžan
eggs	јаја (с мн)	jaja
Enjoy your meal!	Пријатно!	Prijatno!
fats	масти (ж мн)	masti
fig	смоква (ж)	smokva
filling	фил (м)	fil
fish	риба (ж)	riba
flatfish	риба-лист (ж)	riba-list
flour	брашно (с)	brašno
fly agaric	мухомор (м)	muhomor
food	храна (ж)	hrana
fork	виљушка (ж)	viljuška
freshly squeezed juice	цеђени сок (м)	ceđeni sok
fried	пржен	pržen
fried eggs	печена јаја (ж мн)	pečena jaja
frozen	замрзнут	zamrznut
fruit	воћка (ж)	voćka
fruits	воће (с мн)	voće
game	дивљач (ж)	divljač
gammon	димљена шунка (ж)	dimljena šunka
garlic	бели лук, чешњак (м)	beli luk, češnjak
gin	џин (м)	džin
ginger	ђумбир (м)	đumbir
glass	чаша (ж)	čaša
glass	чаша (ж) за вино	čaša za vino
goose	гуска (ж)	guska
gooseberry	огрозд (м)	ogrozd
grain	зрно (с)	zrno
grape	грожђе (с)	grožđe
grapefruit	грејпфрут (м)	grejpfrut

green tea	зелени чај (м)	zeleni čaj
greens	зелениш (м)	zeleniš
halibut	иверак (м)	iverak
ham	шунка (ж)	šunka
hamburger	млевено месо (с)	mleveno meso
hamburger	хамбургер (м)	hamburger
hazelnut	лешник (м)	lešnik
herring	харинга (ж)	haringa
honey	мед (м)	med
horseradish	рен, хрен (м)	ren, hren
hot	врућ	vruć
ice	лед (м)	led
ice-cream	сладолед (м)	sladoled
instant coffee	инстант кафа (ж)	instant kafa
jam	џем (м)	džem
jam	слатко (с)	slatko
juice	сок (м)	sok
kidney bean	пасуљ (м)	pasulj
kiwi	киви (м)	kivi
knife	нож (м)	nož
lamb	јагњетина (ж)	jagnjetina
lemon	лимун (м)	limun
lemonade	лимунада (ж)	limunada
lentil	сочиво (с)	sočivo
lettuce	зелена салата (ж)	zelena salata
light beer	светло пиво (с)	svetlo pivo
liqueur	ликер (м)	liker
liquors	алкохолно пиће (с)	alkoholno piće
liver	џигерица (ж)	džigerica
lunch	ручак (м)	ručak
mackerel	скуша (ж)	skuša
mandarin	мандарина (ж)	mandarina
mango	манго (м)	mango
margarine	маргарин (м)	margarin
marmalade	мармелада (ж)	marmelada
mashed potatoes	пире (м) од кромпира	pire od krompira
mayonnaise	мајонез (м)	majonez
meat	месо (с)	meso
melon	диња (ж)	dinja
menu	јеловник (м)	jelovnik
milk	млеко (с)	mleko
milkshake	милкшејк (м)	milkšejk
millet	просо (с)	proso
mineral water	кисела вода (ж)	kisela voda
morel	смрчак (м)	smrčak
mushroom	гљива, печурка (ж)	gljiva, pečurka
mustard	сенф (м)	senf
non-alcoholic	безалкохолан	bezalkoholan
noodles	резанци (м мн)	rezanci
oats	овас (м)	ovas
olive oil	маслиново уље (с)	maslinovo ulje
olives	маслине (ж мн)	masline

omelet	омлет (м)	omlet
onion	црни лук (м)	crni luk
orange	наранџа (ж)	narandža
orange juice	сок од наранџе (м)	sok od narandže
orange-cap boletus	јасикин турчин (м)	jasikin turčin
oyster	острига (ж)	ostriga
pâté	паштета (ж)	pašteta
papaya	папаја (ж)	papaja
paprika	паприка (м)	paprika
parsley	першун (м)	peršun
pasta	макароне (ж мн)	makarone
pea	грашак (м)	grašak
peach	бресква (ж)	breskva
peanut	кикирики (м)	kikiriki
pear	крушка (ж)	kruška
peel	кора (ж)	kora
perch	гргеч (м)	grgeč
pickled	мариниран, укисељен	mariniran, ukiseljen
pie	пита (ж)	pita
piece	комад (м)	komad
pike	штука (ж)	štuka
pike perch	смуђ (м)	smuđ
pineapple	ананас (м)	ananas
pistachios	пистаћи (мн)	pistaći
pizza	пица (ж)	pica
plate	тањир (м)	tanjir
plum	шљива (ж)	šljiva
poisonous mushroom	отровна печурка (ж)	otrovna pečurka
pomegranate	нар (м)	nar
pork	свињетина (ж)	svinjetina
porridge	каша (ж)	kaša
portion	порција (ж)	porcija
potato	кромпир (м)	krompir
proteins	протеини, беланчевине (мн)	proteini, belančevine
pub, bar	бар (м)	bar
pudding	пудинг (м)	puding
pumpkin	тиква (ж)	tikva
rabbit	зец (м)	zec
radish	ротквица (ж)	rotkvica
raisin	суво грожђе (с)	suvo grožđe
raspberry	малина (ж)	malina
recipe	рецепт (м)	recept
red pepper	црвени бибер (млевени)	crveni biber (mleveni)
red wine	црно вино (с)	crno vino
redcurrant	црвена рибизла (ж)	crvena ribizla
refreshing drink	освежавајуће пиће (с)	osvežavajuće piće
rice	пиринач (м)	pirinač
rum	рум (м)	rum
russula	глувара (ж)	gluvara
rye	раж (ж)	raž

saffron	шафран (м)	šafran
salad	салата (ж)	salata
salmon	лосос (м)	losos
salt	со (ж)	so
salty	слан	slan
sandwich	сендвич (м)	sendvič
sardine	сардина (ж)	sardina
sauce	сос (м)	sos
saucer	тацна (ж)	tacna
sausage	кобасица (ж)	kobasica
seafood	плодови (м мн) мора	plodovi mora
sesame	сусам (м)	susam
shark	ајкула (ж)	ajkula
shrimp	морски рачић (м)	morski račić
side dish	прилог (м)	prilog
slice	парче (с)	parče
smoked	димљен	dimljen
soft drink	безалкохолано пиће (с)	bezalkoholano piće
soup	супа (ж)	supa
soup spoon	супена кашика (ж)	supena kašika
sour cherry	вишња (ж)	višnja
sour cream	кисела павлака (ж)	kisela pavlaka
soy	соја (ж)	soja
spaghetti	шпагети (м мн)	špageti
sparkling	газирана	gazirana
spice	зачин (м)	začin
spinach	спанаћ (м)	spanać
spiny lobster	јастог (м)	jastog
spoon	кашика (ж)	kašika
squid	лигња (ж)	lignja
steak	бифтек (м)	biftek
still	негазирана	negazirana
strawberry	јагода (ж)	jagoda
sturgeon	јесетрина (ж)	jesetrina
sugar	шећер (м)	šećer
sunflower oil	сунцокретово уље (с)	suncokretovo ulje
sweet	сладак	sladak
sweet cherry	трешња (ж)	trešnja
taste, flavor	укус (м)	ukus
tasty	укусан	ukusan
tea	чај (м)	čaj
teaspoon	кашичица (ж)	kašičica
tip	бакшиш (м)	bakšiš
tomato	парадајз (м)	paradajz
tomato juice	сок (м) од парадајза	sok od paradajza
tongue	језик (м)	jezik
toothpick	чачкалица (ж)	čačkalica
trout	пастрмка (ж)	pastrmka
tuna	туњевина (ж)	tunjevina
turkey	ћуран (м)	ćuran
turnip	репа (ж)	repa
veal	телетина (ж)	teletina

vegetable oil	зејтин (м)	zejtin
vegetables	поврће (с)	povrće
vegetarian	вегетаријанац (м)	vegetarijanac
vegetarian	вегетаријански	vegetarijanski
vermouth	вермут (м)	vermut
vienna sausage	виршла (ж)	viršla
vinegar	сирће (с)	sirće
vitamin	витамин (м)	vitamin
vodka	водка (ж)	vodka
waffles	облатне (мн)	oblatne
waiter	конобар (м)	konobar
waitress	конобарица (ж)	konobarica
walnut	орах (м)	orah
water	вода (ж)	voda
watermelon	лубеница (ж)	lubenica
wheat	пшеница (ж)	pšenica
whiskey	виски (м)	viski
white wine	бело вино (с)	belo vino
wild strawberry	шумска јагода (ж)	šumska jagoda
wine	вино (с)	vino
wine list	винска карта (ж)	vinska karta
with ice	са ледом	sa ledom
yogurt	јогурт (м)	jogurt
zucchini	тиквица (ж)	tikvica

Serbian-English gastronomic glossary

авокадо (м)	avokado	avocado
ајкула (ж)	ajkula	shark
алкохолно пиће (с)	alkoholno piće	liquors
ананас (м)	ananas	pineapple
анис (м)	anis	anise
аперитив (м)	aperitiv	aperitif
апетит (м)	apetit	appetite
артичока (ж)	artičoka	artichoke
атлантски лосос (м)	atlantski losos	Atlantic salmon
бадем (м)	badem	almond
бакалар (м)	bakalar	cod
бакшиш (м)	bakšiš	tip
банана (ж)	banana	banana
бар (м)	bar	pub, bar
бармен (м)	barmen	bartender
безалкохолан	bezalkoholan	non-alcoholic
безалкохолано пиће (с)	bezalkoholano piće	soft drink
беланце (с)	belance	egg white
бели лук, чешњак (м)	beli luk, češnjak	garlic
бело вино (с)	belo vino	white wine
бисквити (м мн)	biskviti	cookies
бифтек (м)	biftek	steak
бобица (ж)	bobica	berry
бобице (ж мн)	bobice	berries
бомбона (ж)	bombona	candy
боровница (ж)	borovnica	bilberry
босиљак (м)	bosiljak	basil
брашно (с)	brašno	flour
брезов дед (м)	brezov ded	birch bolete
бресква (ж)	breskva	peach
броколи (м)	brokoli	broccoli
брусница (ж)	brusnica	cowberry
буљон (м)	buljon	clear soup
вадичеп (м)	vadičep	corkscrew
вегетаријанац (м)	vegetarijanac	vegetarian
вегетаријански	vegetarijanski	vegetarian
вермут (м)	vermut	vermouth
вечера (ж)	večera	dinner
виљушка (ж)	viljuška	fork
вино (с)	vino	wine
винска карта (ж)	vinska karta	wine list
виршла (ж)	viršla	vienna sausage
виски (м)	viski	whiskey
витамин (м)	vitamin	vitamin

вишња (ж)	višnja	sour cherry
вода (ж)	voda	water
вода (ж) за пиће	voda za piće	drinking water
водка (ж)	vodka	vodka
воће (с мн)	voće	fruits
воћка (ж)	voćka	fruit
вргањ (м)	vrganj	cep
врућ	vruć	hot
газирана	gazirana	carbonated
газирана	gazirana	sparkling
глувара (ж)	gluvara	russula
гљива, печурка (ж)	gljiva, pečurka	mushroom
говедина (ж)	govedina	beef
горак	gorak	bitter
грашак (м)	grašak	pea
гргеч (м)	grgeč	perch
грејпфрут (м)	grejpfrut	grapefruit
грожђе (с)	grožđe	grape
гума (ж) за жвакање	guma za žvakanje	chewing gum
гуска (ж)	guska	goose
деверика (ж)	deverika	bream
десерт (м)	desert	dessert
дивљач (ж)	divljač	game
дијета (ж)	dijeta	diet
димљен	dimljen	smoked
димљена шунка (ж)	dimljena šunka	gammon
диња (ж)	dinja	melon
додатак, зачин (м)	dodatak, začin	condiment
доручак (м)	doručak	breakfast
ђумбир (м)	đumbir	ginger
житарице (ж мн)	žitarice	cereal grains
житарице (ж мн)	žitarice	cereal crops
жуманце (с)	žumance	egg yolk
замрзнут	zamrznut	frozen
зачин (м)	začin	spice
зејтин (м)	zejtin	vegetable oil
зелена салата (ж)	zelena salata	lettuce
зелени чај (м)	zeleni čaj	green tea
зелениш (м)	zeleniš	greens
зец (м)	zec	rabbit
зрно (с)	zrno	grain
иверак (м)	iverak	halibut
инстант кафа (ж)	instant kafa	instant coffee
јабука (ж)	jabuka	apple
јагњетина (ж)	jagnjetina	lamb
јагода (ж)	jagoda	strawberry
јаја (с мн)	jaja	eggs
јаје (с)	jaje	egg
јасикин турчин (м)	jasikin turčin	orange-cap boletus
јастог (м)	jastog	spiny lobster
јегуља (ж)	jegulja	eel
језик (м)	jezik	tongue

јело (с)	jelo	course, dish
јеловник (м)	jelovnik	menu
јесетрина (ж)	jesetrina	sturgeon
јестива печурка (ж)	jestiva pečurka	edible mushroom
јечам (м)	ječam	barley
јогурт (м)	jogurt	yogurt
кавијар (м)	kavijar	caviar
кајсија (ж)	kajsija	apricot
калорија (ж)	kalorija	calorie
капућино (м)	kapućino	cappuccino
каранфил (м)	karanfil	cloves
карфиол (м)	karfiol	cauliflower
кафа (ж)	kafa	coffee
кафа (ж) са млеком	kafa sa mlekom	coffee with milk
каша (ж)	kaša	porridge
кашика (ж)	kašika	spoon
кашичица (ж)	kašičica	teaspoon
киви (м)	kivi	kiwi
кикирики (м)	kikiriki	peanut
ким (м)	kim	caraway
кисела вода (ж)	kisela voda	mineral water
кисела павлака (ж)	kisela pavlaka	sour cream
клас (м)	klas	ear
кобасица (ж)	kobasica	sausage
кокосов орах (м)	kokosov orah	coconut
коктел (м)	koktel	cocktail
колач (м)	kolač	cake
комад (м)	komad	piece
кондензовано млеко (с)	kondenzovano mleko	condensed milk
конзервирана храна (ж)	konzervirana hrana	canned food
конобар (м)	konobar	waiter
конобарица (ж)	konobarica	waitress
коњак (м)	konjak	cognac
кора (ж)	kora	peel
кориандер (м)	koriander	coriander
краставац (м)	krastavac	cucumber
крем (м)	krem	buttercream
кромпир (м)	krompir	potato
крушка (ж)	kruška	pear
куван	kuvan	boiled
кукуруз (м)	kukuruz	corn
кукуруз (м)	kukuruz	corn
кукурузне пахуљице (ж мн)	kukuruzne pahuljice	cornflakes
купина (ж)	kupina	blackberry
купус (м)	kupus	cabbage
кухиња (ж)	kuhinja	cuisine
лед (м)	led	ice
лешник (м)	lešnik	hazelnut
лигња (ж)	lignja	squid
ликер (м)	liker	liqueur
лимун (м)	limun	lemon

лимунада (ж)	limunada	lemonade
лисичарка (ж)	lisičarka	chanterelle
ловор (м)	lovor	bay leaf
лосос (м)	losos	salmon
лубеница (ж)	lubenica	watermelon
мајонез (м)	majonez	mayonnaise
макароне (ж мн)	makarone	pasta
малина (ж)	malina	raspberry
манго (м)	mango	mango
мандарина (ж)	mandarina	mandarin
маргарин (м)	margarin	margarine
мариниран, укисељен	mariniran, ukiseljen	pickled
мармелада (ж)	marmelada	marmalade
маслац (м)	maslac	butter
маслине (ж мн)	masline	olives
маслиново уље (с)	maslinovo ulje	olive oil
масти (ж мн)	masti	fats
маховница (ж)	mahovnica	cranberry
махунарке (ж мн)	mahunarke	beans
мед (м)	med	honey
месо (с)	meso	meat
милкшејк (м)	milkšejk	milkshake
мирођија (ж)	mirođija	dill
млевено месо (с)	mleveno meso	hamburger
млеко (с)	mleko	milk
морски рак (м)	morski rak	crab
морски рачић (м)	morski račić	shrimp
мрва (ж)	mrva	crumb
мухомор (м)	muhomor	fly agaric
нар (м)	nar	pomegranate
наранџа (ж)	narandža	orange
негазирана	negazirana	still
нож (м)	nož	knife
облатне (мн)	oblatne	waffles
овас (м)	ovas	oats
огрозд (м)	ogrozd	gooseberry
омлет (м)	omlet	omelet
орах (м)	orah	walnut
освежавајуће пиће (с)	osvežavajuće piće	refreshing drink
острига (ж)	ostriga	oyster
отварач (м)	otvarač	bottle opener
отварач (м)	otvarač	can opener
отровна гљива (ж)	otrovna gljiva	death cap
отровна печурка (ж)	otrovna pečurka	poisonous mushroom
павлака (ж)	pavlaka	cream
папаја (ж)	papaja	papaya
паприка (ж)	paprika	bell pepper
паприка (м)	paprika	paprika
парадајз (м)	paradajz	tomato
парче (с)	parče	slice
пастрмка (ж)	pastrmka	trout
пасуљ (м)	pasulj	kidney bean

патка (ж)	patka	duck
паукус (м)	paukus	aftertaste
паштета (ж)	pašteta	pâté
першун (м)	peršun	parsley
печена jaja (ж мн)	pečena jaja	fried eggs
пиво (с)	pivo	beer
пилетина (ж)	piletina	chicken
пире (м) од кромпира	pire od krompira	mashed potatoes
пиринач (м)	pirinač	rice
пистаћи (мн)	pistaći	pistachios
пита (ж)	pita	pie
пица (ж)	pica	pizza
плави патлиџан (м)	plavi patlidžan	eggplant
плодови (м мн) мора	plodovi mora	seafood
поврће (с)	povrće	vegetables
порција (ж)	porcija	portion
посластичарски производи (м мн)	poslastičarski proizvodi	confectionery
предјело (с)	predjelo	appetizer
пржен	pržen	fried
Пријатно!	Prijatno!	Enjoy your meal!
прилог (м)	prilog	side dish
прокељ (м)	prokelj	Brussels sprouts
просо (с)	proso	millet
протеини, беланчевине (мн)	proteini, belančevine	proteins
пудинг (м)	puding	pudding
пшеница (ж)	pšenica	wheat
раж (ж)	raž	rye
ракови (м мн)	rakovi	crustaceans
рачун (м)	račun	check
резанци (м мн)	rezanci	noodles
рен, хрен (м)	ren, hren	horseradish
репа (ж)	repa	turnip
рецепт (м)	recept	recipe
риба (ж)	riba	fish
риба-лист (ж)	riba-list	flatfish
ротквица (ж)	rotkvica	radish
рум (м)	rum	rum
ручак (м)	ručak	lunch
са ледом	sa ledom	with ice
салата (ж)	salata	salad
сардина (ж)	sardina	sardine
светло пиво (с)	svetlo pivo	light beer
свињетина (ж)	svinjetina	pork
сендвич (м)	sendvič	sandwich
сенф (м)	senf	mustard
сир (м)	sir	cheese
сирће (с)	sirće	vinegar
скуша (ж)	skuša	mackerel
сладак	sladak	sweet
сладолед (м)	sladoled	ice-cream

слан	slan	salty
сланина (ж)	slanina	bacon
слатко (с)	slatko	jam
смоква (ж)	smokva	fig
смрчак (м)	smrčak	morel
смуђ (м)	smuđ	pike perch
со (ж)	so	salt
соја (ж)	soja	soy
сок (м)	sok	juice
сок (м) од парадајза	sok od paradajza	tomato juice
сок од наранџе (м)	sok od narandže	orange juice
сом (м)	som	catfish
сос (м)	sos	sauce
сочиво (с)	sočivo	lentil
спанаћ (м)	spanać	spinach
суво грожђе (с)	suvo grožđe	raisin
сунцокретово уље (с)	suncokretovo ulje	sunflower oil
супа (ж)	supa	soup
супена кашика (ж)	supena kašika	soup spoon
сусам (м)	susam	sesame
сушен	sušen	dried
тамно пиво (с)	tamno pivo	dark beer
тањир (м)	tanjir	plate
тацна (ж)	tacna	saucer
телетина (ж)	teletina	veal
тиква (ж)	tikva	pumpkin
тиквица (ж)	tikvica	zucchini
торта (ж)	torta	cake
трешња (ж)	trešnja	sweet cherry
туњевина (ж)	tunjevina	tuna
ћуран (м)	ćuran	turkey
угљени хидрати (м мн)	ugljeni hidrati	carbohydrates
укус (м)	ukus	taste, flavor
укусан	ukusan	tasty
урма (ж)	urma	date
фил (м)	fil	filling
хамбургер (м)	hamburger	hamburger
харинга (ж)	haringa	herring
хељда (ж)	heljda	buckwheat
хладан	hladan	cold
хлеб (м)	hleb	bread
храна (ж)	hrana	food
цвекла (ж)	cvekla	beetroot
цеђени сок (м)	ceđeni sok	freshly squeezed juice
целер (м)	celer	celery
цимет (м)	cimet	cinnamon
црвена рибизла (ж)	crvena ribizla	redcurrant
црвени бибер (млевени)	crveni biber (mleveni)	red pepper
црна кафа (ж)	crna kafa	black coffee
црна рибизла (ж)	crna ribizla	blackcurrant
црни бибер (м)	crni biber	black pepper

црни лук (м)	crni luk	onion
црни чај (м)	crni čaj	black tea
црно вино (с)	crno vino	red wine
чај (м)	čaj	tea
чачкалица (ж)	čačkalica	toothpick
чаша (ж)	čaša	glass
чаша (ж) за вино	čaša za vino	glass
чоколада (ж)	čokolada	chocolate
чоколадан	čokoladan	chocolate
џем (м)	džem	jam
џигерица (ж)	džigerica	liver
џин (м)	džin	gin
шампањац (м)	šampanjac	champagne
шаран (м)	šaran	carp
шаргарепа (ж)	šargarepa	carrot
шафран (м)	šafran	saffron
шећер (м)	šećer	sugar
шљива (ж)	šljiva	plum
шоља (ж)	šolja	cup
шпагети (м мн)	špageti	spaghetti
шпаргла (ж)	špargla	asparagus
штука (ж)	štuka	pike
шумска јагода (ж)	šumska jagoda	wild strawberry
шунка (ж)	šunka	ham

17993410R00117

Printed in Great Britain
by Amazon